An Outline of Psychotherapy

for Medical Students and Practitioners

An Outline of Psychotherapy

for Medical Students and Practitioners

Edited by

Harold Maxwell, MD, FRCPsych

Consultant Psychotherapist and Hon. Senior Lecturer,
West Middlesex Hospital and Charing Cross Hospital.
Member of the British Psychoanalytical Society.

With a foreword by

Steven R. Hirsch, BA, MD, MPhil, FRCP, FRCPsych

Professor of Psychiatry,
Charing Cross Hospital Medical School,
University of London.

WRIGHT

1986 Bristol

Published under the Wright imprint by
IOP Publishing Limited,
Techno House, Redcliffe Way,
Bristol BS1 6NX, England.

British Library Cataloguing in Publication Data

Maxwell, Harold
    An outline of psychotherapy for students and practitioners
    1. Psychotherapy
    I. Title
    616.89'14   RC480

    ISBN 0-7236-0849-0

Typeset by Activity Limited,
Salisbury, Wiltshire

Printed in Great Britain by
Henry Ling Ltd,
The Dorset Press,
Dorchester

To Ch.

With love

Preface

If then our judgment be so de-
praved, our reason overruled, (our)
will precipitated, that we cannot
seek our own good, or moderate
ourselves, as to melancholia commonly it is, the best way for ease is
to impart our misery to some
friend, not to smother it up in our
own breast; for grief concealed
strangles the soul, but when as we
shall impart it to some discreet
trusty loving friend, it is instantly
removed, for a friend's counsel is a
charm; like mandrake wine it
allayeth all our cares.

*'The Anatomie of Melancholie',
1621, by Robert Burton*

I make no apology for putting together in one volume an assemblage of
my own main professional interests, psychoanalysis, psychotherapy and
liaison medicine.

Psychotnerapy is about people and their feelings. There is no line
separating patients, doctors and medical students. At the same time,
while not everyone becomes, say, a bronchitic, a diabetic, or has a baby,
everyone will at various times experience grief, sadness, elation, envy,
fear, paranoia, sleep disturbances, rage and muddled thoughts concerning
the problems of living and relating; all these constitute the very stuff of
psychiatry and also of this book. Incidentally, it would not have found a
market within the world of the medical establishment when I qualified in
1950. Today's mores are, however, thankfully different, being exemplified
by the remark of a young male trainee general practitioner who said in a
recent seminar, "Of course in certain circumstances I would feel it natural
to hold the hand of, or even put my arm around, a patient, male or female,
if in doing so I felt that it would comfort them ...". The other members of
the seminar nodded.

The book was designed with all clinicians in mind, but medical students
and other beginners may find it particularly helpful to refer initially to
Chapters 1 and 3 as a basis.

It is a pleasure to acknowledge my thanks to the contributors to this book, also to the publishers, and to the Aberdeen University Press for allowing Dr. Alexander's chapter to appear, the latter being an extended version of that published in *Models for Psychotherapy* by J.D.H. Haldane, D.A. Alexander and L.G.W. Walker. My wife Marianne kindly read the proofs and made many helpful suggestions.

London, December 1985   H.M.

Contributors

David Alexander, PhD
Senior Lecturer in Mental Health, University of Aberdeen.

Jonathan Sklar, MB, BS, MRCPsych
Consultant Psychotherapist, Addenbrooke's Hospital, Cambridge.

Chris Thomas, MB, BS, MRCP, MRCPsych
Consultant Liaison Psychiatrist, Leicester Royal Infirmary.

Andrew Elder, MB, BS, MRCGP
General Practitioner, London.

Dick Blackwell, BSc
Member of the Institute of Group Analysis.

Alan Cooklin, MB, ChB, FRCPsych
Consultant Family Psychiatrist, Marlborough Day Hospital, London.

Alan King, BSc, MB, ChB, MRCPsych
Consultant Behavioural Psychotherapist, Leicester Royal Infirmary.

Contents

Foreword

By **Steven Hirsch**

Medical students generally enjoy their period as a
student in psychiatry, though they do not expect to
do so. Most doctors going through medical school
only a half generation before had less exposure to
the specialty. For both generations the word
psychotherapy remains one they have heard of and,
nowadays, they may have experienced the subject
transiently as a member of a seminar group, but this
is rarely satisfactory. As teachers of psychiatry, we
continue to be asked for something about
psychotherapy which is didactic and direct —
something which can be written down, thought
about and studied. But chapters in text books are too
short to convey the breadth, depth and relevance of
the approach, and books written for the committed
tend to be too narrow or too ambitious. For an
answer to the questions, 'What is psychotherapy?'
'How does it work?', 'What does it consist of?' this
little book gets it about right. It is not too long to read
in one or two evenings, or too detailed to lose the
reader's interest. It covers the field broadly from
psychoanalytically-based therapy to family systems
theory and conditioning-based behaviour therapy.
The main psychoanalytic concepts are nicely
summarized and clearly defined and there is an
insightful chapter on what happens to the medical
student's feelings as a novice actor in the arena of
acute medicine. The possibility for the physician in
general practice or any specialty to make use of a
psychotherapeutic sixth sense which will help in the
management of his patients is explored in a chapter
on liaison psychiatry, and in another on general

practice. This is a very down-to-earth and practical book which should be useful for anyone who wants to know something of how psychotherapy works and what it has to offer. It will be relevant to those outside the medical profession and in related fields, such as social work, as well as for those within.

It is not, of course, a matter of chance that this book appears at this time. While general psychiatry was maturing and developing clinical and scientific credibility, it had little time for this area of endeavour which is not necessarily medical, and in which scientific hypotheses which test research are still scant. The lack of such research is the fault of its devotees who, for too long, have clung to early concepts which have heuristic value, but need translation into verifiable operational concepts that can be recognized as right or wrong. One problem has been the unwillingness of psychotherapists and analysts to test the effectiveness of their treatment by criteria which lie outside their field of theoretical discourse, such as return to work, resumption of sexual activity, lessening of anxiety and depression scores, lower relapse rates or, in the case of liaison psychiatry, improvement in the patients' physical functioning. Yet, recent studies have begun to show that psychotherapy is a powerful technique by these criteria. Another reason for the dearth of research is that practitioners are, rightfully to some extent, convinced by their own experience — because they almost all undergo therapy as a requisite to training. The training is long, arduous and expensive and the commitment of most therapists once trained is to their patients and to the exercize of their long-won skills; they experience research as antithetical to all this. Fortunately, there is a small but growing number of psychotherapy research workers who are beginning to demonstrate the efficacy of psycother-apy and earn its respect as a bona fide treatment within medicine.

This book is timely because we are witnessing today an exploding interest in psychotherapy on the part of the public and a growing appreciation by the medical profession at all levels of what it has to offer. This may reflect an increasing standard of living for those in society who expect more for themselves and are less willing to tolerate inner turmoil and difficulties in their relationships with others.

Though our own Department of Psychiatry at Charing Cross is biologically-orientated in research, and community-orientated from a service point of view, we require all our psychiatrists in training to obtain experience in psychotherapy, because we believe the skills are essential if one wants to address oneself fully to a patient's treatment. This concern is also reflected in recent changes in the membership examinations of the Royal College of Psychiatry. Similarly, our medical students are all being given an opportunity to treat a patient psychotherapeutically, if they wish, and there is now a liaison psychiatry and psychotherapy service throughout our hospital which is appreciated by physicians, surgeons and obstetricians alike.

The growing demand by the public for 'humanistic medicine' and the increasing interest in fringe medicine of all sorts is further evidence of this new ethic. If doctors can begin even as medical students to guard against the erosion of that sensitivity and human interest they have before they even enter an anatomy room, and go on to develop the skills which will enable them to use these qualities as they carry out their medical work, the demand for fringe medicine will be kept at bay. This primer is a very good starting point for such a task.

1

Psychotherapy: A General Introduction

by Harold Maxwell

The content of this volume pertains to psychotherapy by *medical personnel*, including students. It is necessary, however, to note that unlike medicine, psychotherapy *per se* is a completely unregistered profession and consequently there is no body like the General Medical Council responsible for the activities of psychotherapists. Certain members of several core professions, e.g. psychiatry, psychology, nursing and social work, all practise psychotherapy and when doing so are answerable to their own professional bodies. There are, however, other psychotherapists who have trained in various ways, and may not necessarily have a background in one of the caring professions. Some of these people will belong to professional organisations such as the British Psycho-Analytic Society, the Society for Analytical Psychology and the British Association of Psychotherapists, though anyone can in fact call himself a 'psychotherapist' or even 'psychoanalyst'.

Nevertheless, a significant number of persons seeking help from psychotherapy will turn to members of the medical profession because of the status of the latter, which still enjoys a remarkable degree of trust on the part of the general public. Medical personnel who are psychotherapists will usually have been trained as general psychiatrists and in addition followed courses leading to membership of one of the three bodies referred to above. As far as other medical personnel are concerned, to some extent it will be the degree of *involvement* with the patient, both in intensity and duration, which will affect the 'depth' of the physician's influence. Those with minimum involvement would naturally include, say, clinical pathologists and radiologists, while at the other end of the spectrum would be the family doctor with his 'permanent' relationship and the general psychiatrist. In between would be every specialist category pertaining to clinical work.

Nowadays, there seems to be a greater emphasis placed on what has come to be called the doctor-patient relationship in general medicine and surgery, dermatology, obstetrics and, especially, gynaecology. The *family practitioner's* use of psychotherapy is covered elsewhere (Chapter 5), while the *general psychiatrist* will involve himself in supportive and insight-directed psychotherapy, to an extent varying with his own inclinations, in this way supplementing his physical and social measures in the total management of patients.

In the sphere of both general and psychiatric practice the teaching of **Michael Balint**, which is also discussed elsewhere, will be remembered with its credo of the doctor/patient relationship. Naturally this factor had been known long before Balint described it, but was never so well delineated in practical terms. In this context, a remarkable paper by Houston (1939) just before the second world war, emphasized the placebo effect of the doctor himself as a therapeutic agent. The point was made that throughout history the number of pharmacological preparations with a 'genuine' and predictable action was extremely small and the 'greatness' of physicians, up to effectively the 19th or even 20th century, depended upon the *personality* of that physician and its placebo effect, (that is, the faith evoked in the efficacy of the doctor's personality). Hypnosis and other modern, 'popular' procedures without phsyiological validation are based on the same mechanism.

● Principles of Individual Therapy

What is psychotherapy?
It is a professional way of dealing with human misery and unhappiness, including psychiatric states, by the interaction of the patient with one or more people. It can be individual, group, marital or family. The most usual method of interaction is through talk and the psychotherapy which ensues may, as already noted, be supportive or insightful, the latter hopefully leading to development of the personality. Psychotherapy in the context of this book is concerned with clinical practice: it may or may not be used in combination with physical methods of treatment such as drugs.

Where?
The setting is extremely important. Its degree of opulence does not matter, its *constancy* does. Usually a small or medium-sized room, quietly furnished with the absence of distractions of, say, the telephone, with both patient and therapist being physically comfortable.

Who?
The psychotherapist is a professional, for our purposes a physician. He will have had at least some training, may belong to one of the so-called 'schools' of psychotherapy and probably have had some personal therapy or analysis.

● Features of Psychotherapy

Generally, psychotherapy will be either *supportive*, that is, 'encouraging the positive', or will hopefully enable the patient to gain *insight* into how and why factors from the past have determined his present predicament and how to a large extent he is compelled to repeat past patterns of inexpedient behaviour.

With the start of treatment, the patient will by implication and at the very least, receive the message that he is 'worthy of help' and thereby experience enhancement to his self-esteem. The installation and maintenance of *hope* will also be a feature, which will be compounded by the constancy of the setting and of the therapist himself. The latter cannot delegate his role to a locum or deputy: *psychotherapy is above all based upon a human relationship*.

The initial interview

This is partly a fact-finding process but will differ from a medical model interview in so far that, in addition to facts such as name, address, occupation etc., the patient's demeanour, dress and general attitudes will be noted. The overall mood that the patient evokes in the therapist is also important, especially in coming to an 'empathetic' diagnosis. The more adept and experienced the practitioner, the more accurate will be his antennae in receiving emotional messages from the patient.

The psychotherapy sessions

What takes place? Apart from implicit messages of support which are conveyed to the patient, *facilitation* is provided by the therapist by means of his interest, recognition and sense of receptiveness. *Confrontation* is also used as a means of making the patient aware of a reaction that has been provoked within the therapist. *Reassurance*, suggestion and direction are also employed, as is questioning, though the last should be used sparingly. *Interpretations* are means of conveying to the patient an understanding on the part of the therapist, whereby something which is implied or hidden from the patient's consciousness may be brought to his attention. Interpretations sometimes involve the therapist, when they are called transference interpretations and as such are especially pertinent to orthodox psychoanalysis. *Advice* and *guidance* are also given, as well as reinforcement and behaviour modification. The last is conveyed to the patient by tacit approval, or otherwise, of the patient's activities, statements or decisions. *Silence* may be a problem to psychotherapists in training. It is of several kinds and the over-riding mood will hopefully be picked up: hostile, neutral or restful. A therapeutic step forward during a silence would be for the therapist to say to the patient something like, "I feel a bit lost and don't really know what to say" or "I'm confused and rather muddled and I wonder whether you feel the same". This will be a truism and will enable the patient to feel recognised and understood even if it is only in a 'negative' way, so that the basis may be laid for future, naturally more positive experiences.

Supportive psychotherapy

This is the minimum type of psychotherapy. Evidence of goodwill, consistency and sincere interest are conveyed with an implicit promise that the patient with all his fears, weaknesses, anxieties and above all his aggressiveness, will be received and contained by the therapist. As its name suggests, this psychotherapy is especially called for to support the patient during acute or long-standing periods of crisis. Clear-cut events such as bereavements or divorces may, for a given period of time, call for regular meetings with the patient so that the situations can be worked through and he may gradually come to terms with the situations. Those with a low threshold to life's exigencies may need, in the extreme, a lifelong availability on the part of the therapist, who ideally will combine this role with that of family doctor. The very fact that the latter 'is there' may often be sufficient to prevent many patients breaking down. The good GP has, in fact, had transferred to him aspects of a good parent, who will not condemn or judge, but will stay and be available. Non-medical counsellors are now being trained in considerable numbers to deal with the common-or-garden problems of living which many patients just cannot cope with and which in the past were dealt with by the priest, lawyer or lord of the manor.

Insight psychotherapy

This is a process whereby the patient is encouraged to understand that habitual 'defences' (*qv*) and methods of reacting to external situations may be inappropriate and unpropitious, often provoking other people. Hopefully, their origin in early life will be understood by both patient and therapist and conscious attempts at modification and change will be made. The use of dreams, slips of the tongue and ruminative free association of speech will be part of the process. Here the aim is more ambitious than in supportive psychotherapy. The patient will be helped to understand that certain patterns of responses to the environment are self-defeating, leading to further negative situations. This type of therapy is a way of showing a patient how he can, through reflection and given sufficient motivation, react with different patterns of behaviour. It is an experience based on psychoanalysis, and a certain amount of personal therapy for the doctor may be necessary in order to enable the therapist to distinguish between his own 'hang-ups' and those of the patient.

It used to be thought by the early psychoanalysts that the aim of treatment was to 'make the unconscious, conscious'. Nowadays, one would hope that the degree of suffering by the individual may be reduced as a result of *integration*, that is, the coming together and acceptance of various contradictory feelings and attitudes: that the 'pain' of these *ambivalences* will gradually lessen and become tolerable, so that maturing and positive processes will supervene, thus reducing the need for painful and costly defences to be employed with suffering for the person, his family or even society as a whole.

- **Clinical Conditions Where Psychotherapy May Be Considered**
1. Supportive psychotherapy may be indicated when any of life's crises affecting the person or his family are being negotiated, e.g. divorce, redundancy, retirement, bereavement.
2. Psychiatric conditions, especially recurring states of baseless anxiety or depression. Addictions. Some of the schizophrenic illnesses.
3. 'Existential conditions' — probably the commonest situations that particularly the specialist is nowadays called upon to treat. The symptomotology is vague, confused, alters from day to day and accounts for an ill-defined ennui whereby both isolation (loneliness) and its opposite, the too-invasive and too-close proximity of another person are felt to be intolerable, so that an oscillation of depressive aloneness and suffocating relatedness is experienced, accounting for *difficulties in relationships*, with

perhaps recourse to drugs and alcohol. Sexual problems of all types are included in this section.

4.   Some medical states of an episodic or chronic nature, e.g.:
Migraine
Asthma
Musculo-skeletal diseases
Gastrointestinal symptoms

These conversion phenomena or psychosomatic conditions are usually very resistant to change by psychotherapy — frequently, they are best left to sympathetic management by the general physician or family doctor.

Factors to be considered in evaluating the suitability for psychotherapy

1. Motivation
This will depend on the degree of real (mental) suffering or distress, usually anxiety and/or depression, and the determination to find a better *modus vivendi*.

2. Age
Age is not as important as perhaps might be imagined. Both the very young and the elderly can be helped.

3. 'Ego strength'
This means the general cohesiveness and state of maturity of the personality, as shown by attainments in general; the sources of happiness, if any; and, above all, the ability or otherwise to *sustain* relationships both in the personal life and in a work situation.

4. Intelligence
A minimum is certainly necessary but again this factor need not be over-emphasized. More important is the capacity or otherwise for insight, i.e. the presence of 'psychological mindedness', and above all the motivation for change.

5. The ability to tolerate anxiety and frustration
This is important, as psychotherapy is often a slow process, not enjoying the instant relief that medication can often provide for symptoms. A history of 'acting out', that is the involvement of the patient in unpropitious or destructive activities, is a sign that psychotherapy may be especially difficult.

6. 'Secondary gain'
This means, for instance, that by the maintenance of symptoms the patient may exercise considerable control over his environment, sometimes in a blackmailing way.

7. Reality factors
These include the availability of specialists, the willingness of the patient to invest time and sometimes money in his treatment and, ideally, a family situation which is objective towards psychotherapy.

8. *Types of defences*

If it seems that excessive denial, splitting, confusion or projection are employed, it will suggest that psychotherapy will be difficult, as would evidence of acting out (poor impulse control) or psychosomatic disease.

● **Psychoanalysis**

This is a special method of psychotherapy invented by Freud, dealing especially with transference (*qv*). This special relationship which develops between a patient and the analyst is analysed and traced back to the patient's earliest relationships. While most other forms of psychotherapy are based on suggestion and encouragement, psychoanalysis is concerned with the largely unconsciously-derived and transferred feelings and attitudes with which the patient invests the analyst. This transference is to some extent fostered by the analyst, who remains relatively 'anonymous'.

Some important psychoanalytic concepts
Defences

These are universal phenomena and must be respected. The 'defence' is against overwhelming *internal* anxiety, as opposed to 'real' or outside, physical dangers. It is important to grasp that there is an internal world as well as an external world and that the former does in fact determine many of our basic moods, responses, feelings, attitudes and, in a psychiatric sense, the types of *distortions* which may make human relationships difficult or even impossible. These distortions, especially towards other people, are based on attitudes to important figures from the past, often evoking difficulties which may never have been resolved, thus perpetuating feelings which, even at the time, may well have been inappropriate to the event taking place (*see* Transference).

It must be realized that it is only when these mechanisms become exaggerated or habitual, that they can be called pathologic and, paradoxically, it is when they break down completely that psychiatric symptoms begin. Were it not for defence mechanisms, which automatically come into play when we meet with any unpleasant reality, life would soon become a burden, if not impossible. Such defences include:

a. Denial This is a way whereby unpleasant events may conveniently be 'blotted out'. Examples would include the pain of a recent bereavement, an unpleasant sight consequent upon an accident or other trauma, the usage of the 'sour grapes' phenomenon, (i.e. something which has not, in reality, been available has its value denied). 'Splitting' is often associated with denial. It excludes life's grey areas: everything and everyone is black or white, good or bad, etc.

b. Displacement If hostile feelings or emotions cannot be expressed to authority or other powerful figures, they may be *displaced* on to others less threatening or further away; for instance, it is safe to hate an enemy on the other side of the world. Another example would be kicking the cat to release frustration towards someone whom one could not attack safely.

c. Phobic avoidance Sometimes very primitive and deep-seated situations which evoke intolerable terror become focused on to specific objects or situations in the external world through a process of subtle and unconscious symbolic transformation. Thus, animals or other creatures, e.g. snakes and spiders, or situations such as open spaces or closed rooms, come to *stand for* these very primitive, sincerely 'forgotten' and very basic situations. The important point is how much of an inconvenience it is to avoid the substituted, external symbol of terror, e.g. it is not much of a problem for a snake-phobic living in a suburb of a big city, but a real fear of flying is, perhaps, a constraint for a businessman. (The section on Behavioural Methods will highlight these conditions and their management.)

d. Projection   This is ascribing to others negative feelings and attitudes in ourselves. It is the basis of paranoid states for, if we 'believe' that others are feeling or behaving badly, we are then justified in hating, hurting or attacking them in return.

e. Rationalization   This is a means whereby the true reason for a course of action is hidden by *apparent* explanations.

f. Reaction formation   Denotes going to the opposite extreme towards experiences which may be morally unacceptable, e.g. excessive cleanliness to counteract innate wishes and instincts to be dirty, untruthful, inexact or spontaneous.

g. Regression   Denotes a return to a more childlike state, so that temporarily at least, one is able to re-experience being a child with no responsibilities. Naturally the phenomenon occurs in sleep and it is an acceptable event at times of illness when it is a sort of 'secondary gain'.

h. Repression and suppression   A way of putting off, or burying, painful or even exciting feelings or thoughts. As with all defence mechanisms, if it is too successful it is like 'throwing out the baby with the bathwater' and some people are never able to react appropriately or spontaneously to, say, a traumatic or sexual situation. Such people are somehow 'different' or even experienced as unreal.

i. States of confusion   Indecision and other ruminative states of puzzled vagueness may be a way of distancing ourselves from unpleasant reality. Conflict and ambivalence, which can be painful, may be avoided in this way.

j. Sublimation   This is a so-called 'higher' solution, whereby anxieties become channelled into positive acts or ways of life, e.g. creativity, gardening (say), restoring objects and turning sadism into an occupation such as surgery.

   It is worth repeating that defence mechanisms are present in us all and it is when they break down that symptoms may ensue.

Transference

This is an ubiquitous and everyday phenomenon between persons. Attitudes, feelings and ideas from the past towards significant people become transferred to acquaintances and even friends in the present, often without justification. It is, however, the most important *tool* in psychoanalysis and psychoanalytic psychotherapy, as the patient may invest the therapist with what may well be totally inappropriate characteristics and attitudes, which can be changed or at least modified during the therapy and, by extrapolation, a more realistic appraisal of people in the patient's world may become established. Especially, strangers and acquaintances become less endowed with initial hostility and threat, so that more propitious feelings between the patient and his objects can become established.

Countertransference

This is the equivalent in the therapist. This will include the therapist's blind-spots of which cognisance and knowledge must be present. Its existence makes a personal therapy on the part of the doctor highly desirable, some would say essential. Countertransference feelings can also mirror attitudes, both conscious and unconscious, originating in the patient, but experienced and recognised in the therapist. With proper timing they may be conveyed to the patient as an aid to the two persons' joint understanding.

The unconscious

This refers to both the part of the mind about which the subject is unaware and processes that are not within consciousness. Its existence is suggested by three phenomena:

1. Dreams
2. Post hypnotic suggestion
3. Slips of the tongue

    Unconscious processes are linked to what Freud called primary processes. These are primitive and unstructured methods of mental functioning: they reduce unpleasure or pain and promote *pleasure*. Images become fused and can readily replace and symbolize each other, as in dreams. *Secondary process* thinking, on the other hand, is logical, orderly and bound up with reality, reducing unpleasure or pain by adaptation.

Reference

Houston W. R. (1938) The doctor himself as a therapeutic agent. *Ann. Int. Med.* **11**, 1416–25.

2

Psychodynamic therapy

by David A. Alexander

● **History and Development**

The practice of psychotherapy can be rewarding and demanding, both intellectually and emotionally. Uniquely among the professions, in order to be effective, the psychotherapist often has to 'get involved' personally, at least to some extent. This can be taxing and difficult and, like other specialities dealing with people, its injudicious application can be harmful so that it demands an unusually high degree of personal integrity. Over the last 40 years *schools* of psychotherapy have multiplied in such a way that aspirants to the profession are faced with a bewildering array of approaches.

In the absence of a comprehensive body of convincing empirical data to justify the claims of one school against those of another, it is difficult to decide which theories and techniques to adopt. In fact, despite what we might like to believe, many clinicians ally themselves to a particular form of therapy for motives that have little to do with logic or evaluative research. Powerful determinants of their choice include personal prejudice and serendipity.

Nonetheless, whatever the factors underlying his choice of model, the practitioner should always consider what he is doing to his patients and why. More specifically, he should be in a position to answer five basic questions. The answers to these questions will expose important assumptions underlying his particular choice of therapy. These questions are:

1. What factors influence human behaviour?
2. What are the basic aims of this therapy?
3. What are the characteristic features of the therapeutic relationship?
4. What are the techniques and skills associated with this therapy?
5. What problems or patients can best be helped by this therapy?

In this chapter we will address each of these questions in relation to the psychodynamic model. Before doing so, however, we must look at some of the important historical features of this model in order to form a background against which these questions can be more appropriately considered.

Most forms of psychotherapy almost certainly owe something to Sigmund Freud (1856–1939) and to the treatment called 'psychoanalysis' which he developed and which has served as the prototype for later psychodynamic therapies. This does not mean that Freud 'invented' psychotherapy or that all his ideas were entirely novel. On the contrary, many of his concepts and ideas have very long pedigrees. For instance, the notion of a 'talking cure' (as psychoanalysis has been called), achieved through the verbal expression of pent-up feelings, is closely related to the Catholic 'confessional'. It can also be traced to the use of the theatre in ancient Greece as a public means of 'purging the passions'. However, while it is important to be aware of the ancestry of some of our current ideas and practices, the fact that we can identify their medical and cultural antecedents in no way devalues the signal contribution of Freud and the early analysts. Such has been the indelible and widespread influence of psychoanalytic ideas that they have fertilized developments not only in medical psychology and psychiatry, but also in the social sciences and the arts. Psychoanalysis has offered a form of treatment for cer tain mental disorders as well as a distinctive view of man, his behaviour and his development.

Inevitably, certain features of this widespread movement attracted a good deal of opposition and criticism. Analytical propositions were attacked on the grounds that they were formulated too loosely to be amenable to verification or refutation by traditional scientific procedures. It is hardly surprising that this objection was raised, because the late 19th and early 20th centuries had seen many notable advances in the physical sciences, and 'verifiability' and 'refutability' were acclaimed as the two most important criteria of the integrity and status of a proposition or theory.

Another related criticism was that the 'evidence' offered by clinicians to support their claims was nothing more than unsubstantiated hearsay and anecdotes: it was the product of private activities and experience occurring in the consulting room. Theorists and clinicians espousing other models, the 'Behaviourists' in particular, have consistently argued that those who practise a psychodynamic form of therapy seem to have been reluctant to evaluate the process and outcome of their therapeutic work and to adhere to the conventional canons of scientific enquiry.

Criticisms such as these should not be dismissed readily or be upheld slavishly. There are some major and specific difficulties in carrying out investigative and evaluative research in this area and it is questionable whether the study of human behaviour can be carried out in the same way as one might study, for example, the love life of an amoeba! On the other hand, it cannot be disputed that there is a dearth of studies into the process, concepts and therapeutic values of psychodynamic therapy. There is also a need to remove some of the mystery and veneration which surrounds this form of therapy. Illusory concepts, abstruse reasoning and a pseudo-scientific jargon may be intriguing or even reassuring to some, but such things probably contribute nothing to the welfare of patients or to the development of our understanding of man's behaviour and experience.

Whatever the 'scientific' status of psychoanalysis, however, its significance in the history of Western thought is not in doubt and this fact has much to do with the personal contribution of Freud himself. It is therefore fitting to make some brief reference to his personal and intellectual life.

Despite his enormous contribution to clinical work, Freud was a reluctant therapist and physician. His reasons for embarking on a medical career were more pragmatic than idealistic — being a medical practitioner was more lucrative than being a physiologist — and his ambitions were more academic than humanitarian. His main aim was to produce a general theory of human behaviour and, in pursuit of this aim, he regarded himself firstly as a scientist and only secondly as a clinician. Being a compassionate man by nature, however, Freud did not sacrifice his patients' welfare in the furtherance of his own academic aspirations as a psychologist.

His intellectual integrity, not to say courage, cannot be questioned. Throughout his career he displayed a willingness to let (as he put it) 'facts speak for themselves', even although, in doing so, he had to modify and relinquish some of his most fundamental propositions, such as that about the role of sexual trauma in the development of certain mental disorders. His willingness and, indeed, his determination to adhere to 'the facts' also led him to maintain certain views despite the resultant public and professional criticism and even odium. For example, originally, Freud believed that sexual fantasies and attachments begin in early childhood and that the child obtains sexual satisfaction from different parts of his body as he develops. Moreover, he argued that early childhood sexual experiences continue to exert an effect in later life. When one thinks of the moral straitjacket imposed in the Victorian era on the public discussion of sexual matters, it is hardly surprising that these views met with disbelief and disapproval. A lesser man might easily have succumbed to the strong opposition and have relinquished his ideas; Freud did not.

His courage in holding to or modifying his theory in the light of empirical and clinical evidence was matched by his physical courage. In the last years of his life he was handicapped by a terminal cancer of the jaw, but he continued his academic and clinical work despite this distressing and painful illness. Moreover, in order that he might retain all his mental powers, he refused analgesics for this condition.

It was, however, his shrewdness and sensitivity as an observer of human behaviour that led to major developments in his theory about man. Generally, it was not that he saw different things from other people, but rather that he saw the same things differently. The capacity to reformulate old ideas and synthesize common observations is, of course, the hallmark of the creative and outstanding scientist.

An opportunity to display this ability occurred when he attended the dramatic demonstrations by Dr. Charcot in Paris. The purpose of these demonstrations was to show how patients, in response to hypnotic suggestion, could manifest symptoms which resembled neurological ones such as aphonia, paralysis and paraesthesia. Impressed and puzzled by these demonstrations and yet firmly convinced about the enormous importance of psychological factors, Freud reflected on some of the patients who had been referred to him in Vienna for treatment of similar conditions. He wondered if it might be possible that these symptoms had developed in response to the patients' own unconscious ideas — a form of 'autosuggestion'. He suspected that the patients would have been as unaware of the effect of their own ideas as Charcot's patients had been of his suggestions. Using hypnosis as a means of removing symptoms rather than as a means of inducing them, Freud found that hypnosis was an effective method of directly achieving symptom relief. Despite his initial success, however, he was troubled by the thought that if he and the patient did not know what underlay the development of these symptoms then, while suggestion might produce some relief, it would only be temporary; either the influence of these unconscious ideas would begin to reassert itself and the symptoms would reappear, or other symptoms might emerge in their place. The second possibility has been described as 'symptom substitution'.

It was in the course of working with the Austrian physician Josef Breuer (with whom he wrote, in 1895, the seminal *Studien über Hysterie*) Freud realized that here might be another way of using hypnosis, one which might offer a more durable 'cure' or change. Instead of using hypnosis as a means of achieving direct symptom relief, when the underlying cause remained unknown, Freud began to use it as a means of revealing and exploring what had given rise to the symptom in the first place. The possibility of using hypnosis in this way had been suggested to him by the fact that one of Breuer's patients (immortalized in the literature as 'Anna O') had been able under hypnosis to recall feelings and events previously inaccessible to her and, in doing so, she had been relieved of her symptoms. In brief, therefore, the aim was to treat the underlying cause and not just the symptom, the latter being regarded as a breakthrough, in a disguised form, of 'blocked-off' or inhibited feelings.

At that time, Freud was proposing a radical approach because the prevailing view was a reductionist one: symptoms were held to be due to a disturbance in some physical or biochemical system. Freud, on the other hand, was claiming that many symptoms, physical and mental, had a psychological cause and, moreover, that these symptoms had some personal and symbolic meaning for the patient. The patient, however, is frequently unaware of this meaning or significance, and unaware of the association between his emotions and his symptoms. At this stage, it is interesting to consider how many common expressions and metaphors there are in our language which reflect the association between emotions and parts of the body. These include 'he's a pain in the neck', 'he gets on my nerves', 'you're breaking my heart', 'he's a real headache to me' and 'that was a real body blow'.

It was this belief in the association between the underlying emotions and the overt symptoms that confirmed Freud's opinion that many mental disorders, and in particular the neuroses, could not be understood adequately, or treated successfully, using conventional medical concepts and procedures.

For a number of reasons, Freud gave up his use of hypnosis and developed a procedure known as 'free association', whereby the patient was encouraged to talk without fear of censure about his past experiences and his most private thoughts, wishes, fears and so forth. In their doing so, Freud believed that the patients and he would be able to unravel the connection between underlying but previously unrecognised factors and presenting symptoms. To hold this view, of course, assumes a 'psychological determinism' in that such a view implies that all aspects of behaviour and experience can be seen as outcomes of earlier mental or physical events. According to this view, symptoms do not appear by chance or caprice.

Although this procedure of free association was obviously a much more time-consuming one than hypnosis, Freud believed that the results obtained would be lasting. By helping the patient become aware of events, ideas and feelings, which previously had been unconscious, the effect of these phenomena in terms of symptom development would cease. Moreover, by resolving the underlying problem, symptom-substitution would not occur.

As one might expect, psychoanalysis in particular, and psychodynamic theory in general, have undergone many revisions and modifications since the days of Freud and his contemporaries. Some of these developments will emerge as we address the five basic questions which were raised earlier, and to which we can now turn.

- ### What Factors Influence Human Behaviour?

According to the psychodynamic view of man, our behaviour and experience are the result of a number of competing urges, wishes and other influences, some conscious, but others unconscious and, therefore, beyond our awareness. It is to these unconscious influences that much of psychodynamic therapy is directed. Indeed, one of the most influential concepts in the attempt to understand human behaviour and experience is that of unconscious motivation. Although there has been much debate about whether or not the unconscious is a legitimate concept and worthy of study, much psychological research (including that into 'selective attention' and 'subliminal perception') quite independent of psychodynamic theory has confirmed the need to acknowledge the influence of unconscious processes. In his earliest writings, Freud regarded the unconscious as a sovereign concept: a concept which included memories, impulses and ideas generally not available to conscious scrutiny, and he distinguished the unconscious from the 'preconscious' and the 'conscious'. The former he viewed as the repository of impulses, sense impressions and memories of which we are not immediately aware, but could easily be so if required or if the focus of our attention were suitably redirected. (For example, we are not normally aware of our clothes touching our bodies until something directs our attention to these sensations.) The conscious sphere of mental life, a more self-explanatory concept, corresponds to all which we are aware of at any given time. It also incudes, therefore, those aspects of ourselves to which we are prepared to admit (if only to ourselves), in contrast to those features, for instance of our personality or past, which we find less acceptable and which we reassuredly relegate to the unconscious realm. (Although it is very convenient to talk in terms of the 'unconscious' and 'conscious' as though they had some spatial existence, this may be misleading. It is probably more accurate to think of all mental activity as occurring along a continuum of consciousness, ranging from complete unawareness to focal attentiveness.)

The distinction between conscious and unconscious mental activities is also associated with a differentiation between cognitive processes. The conscious level of functioning involves 'secondary processes', which are logical, rational and geared to meet the demands of the real world. In contrast, unconscious activities are associated with 'primary processes' which are not usually adapted to meet the demands of reality, but rather function to achieve the satisfaction of very basic and urgent needs or drives. We can catch glimpses of these more primitive aspects of ourselves and the processes associated with them, when we are dreaming, are emotionally aroused or are under the influence of alcohol or other drugs. *In vino veritas* is therefore a particularly apt aphorism according to psychodynamic theory. Slips of the tongue and slips of the pen, collectively referred to as 'parapraxes' ('Freudian slips'), may also provide interesting and important clues to the presence of unconscious views, feelings and wishes, many of which we would not comfortably acknowledge in full consciousness. Anyone who is particularly interested in the topic of unconsciously motivated errors should, as well as reflect on his own 'mistakes', read Freud's *The Psychopathology of Everyday Life* (1914).

In the 1920s, Freud revised his ideas about mental activity and its influence on man's experience and behaviour. He offered a new model, a good deal of which still permeates much of our thinking and language, both lay and professional. This model is a more complex one, involving a tripartite division of the psyche into three elements: the Id, the Ego and the Superego. Although it is a more complex model, it has the advantage of trying to embrace biological, experimental, interpersonal and social aspects of human life.

The first of these elements, the Id, represents all the inherited, biological and constitutional features of the individual, including instincts and basic drives, such as those pertaining to eating, aggression, sex and elimination. These forces, Freud believed, operate according to the hedonistic Pleasure Principle in that they avoid being frustrated and seek immediate gratification, regardless of the consequences. On the other hand, the Superego is very much concerned with the consequences of our actions, since it is built up from internalized representations of the standards and ideals upheld by others who are particularly important to us. Living as we do in relationships with others, we have to conform to many social and cultural standards, and it is through the Superego that many of these standards are transmitted and perpetuated. Since we do not like rejection, censure or punishment, we tend to conform to many of the expectations of others, especially those whom we hold in high regard or who have authority over us. For most of us, the first 'culture' to which we are exposed is that of our own family and, consequently, much of our Superego development reflects the impact of parental values and ideals.

The third element, the Ego, roughly corresponds to the conscious level of functioning. It develops progressively from birth — according to some authorities, it does so from an even earlier stage — and its first task is to distinguish between the inner world of subjective experience and external reality; or, to put it another way, it tries to distinguish between 'I' and 'not I'. The Ego is reality-oriented, and it therefore has to find acceptable and appropriate ways of satisfying the demands of the Id, although this means that, at least temporarily, the gratification of the Id must be delayed. For example, if we are ravenously hungry, the Id drives us to find some immediate way of obtaining food, perhaps by theft or deception, but to do so would be socially unacceptable. Realistically, we can see also that it is likely to lead to further difficulties for us: for instance, we might be caught or we might harm others in the process. Thus the Ego tries to ensure that the satisfaction of such a need is sufficiently delayed to allow us to find some reasonable and socially acceptable means of finding food and satisfying the urge to eat. On other occasions, the Ego has to appease the demands of the Superego. Although the Superego can be helpful by keeping us out of trouble (rather like the layman's concept of conscience), it can also act as a source of primitive, irrational and punitive morality and idealism. Consequently, instead of guiding us helpfully, the Superego may unnecessarily restrict and inhibit our behaviour, feelings and personal development. This may be seen in those individuals who are totally dominated by their need to do 'the right thing' and avoid upsetting others.

In other words, the Ego may have to act as an arbiter in the face of the demands of the Id and the Superego: not an easy task, because the demands of one element may be as clamorous, irrational and pressing as those of the other. Sometimes, the effectiveness of the Ego can be substantially reduced or modified by the effects of alcohol, sensory deprivation, insomnia or powerful emotions. Consequently, mental activity, experiences and behaviour occurring during these altered states of awareness appear to be less censored, less rational and more under the influence of the Pleasure Principle. Some dreams may also show the signs of reduced Ego-involvement, and it is not surprising that Freud described dreams as 'the royal road to the unconscious'.

Freud had great difficulty in deciding what were man's basic drives and instincts—a difficulty, we should note, that he shared with most other theorists. He settled for the notion that there were two mainsprings driving man's behaviour: these were the 'life instincts' and the 'death instincts' (conventionally referred to as 'Eros' and 'thanatos' respectively). The latter group he regarded as basically destructive in that they seek to educe us to inorganic matter. The life instincts, on the other hand, try to maintain life: in this capacity, one of these instincts, the sexual instinct, plays a particularly significant role. At first, Freud believed that the sexual instinct was served exclusively by a form of energy called the 'libido', but later he concluded that all life instincts drew from this source.

Although Freud was particularly impressed by the frequency with which conflict occurred over sexual matters, what is more important to note is not the nature of the instincts themselves, but rather their potential for creating competing influences on man's behaviour and thereby providing a source of conflict. In Freud's view, we are constantly being pulled and pushed in different directions by equally powerful but mutually antagonistic forces. Thus, behind man's experience and behaviour, there lies a constantly shifting dynamic of forces among which we are always trying to achievē some equilibrium. As applied to psychology, the term 'dynamic', borrowed from 19th-century physics and physiology, reflects this particular view. Freud was very impressed with the notion of forces competing with one another and he was aware that in physics the resolution of the opposition between two competing forces was sometimes achieved by the emergence of a third force which moves off in a completely different direction from the other two. In terms of human behaviour and experience, the equivalent of the emergence of the third force would be the development of a symptom. According to this theory, symptom formation is not therefore a random or inexplicable event, but a means of relieving what otherwise would be intolerable and interminable conflict, in other words, a compromise, a 'solution' that is the *least unacceptable* to all the forces concerned: Id, Ego and reality.

The importance of the concept of conflict is obvious if we think how often depression, anxiety and physical symptoms, such as headaches, 'low back pain' and stomach upsets, develop when we are racked with doubts involving opposites: 'Will I, won't I?' 'Did I, didn't I?' and 'Can I, can't I?'. There are, of course, many other conflicts whose source may not be obvious to us; the conflict remains at an unconscious level and we only become aware of the symptoms to which it has given rise.

Some conflicts may be quite transient, others may trouble us throughout our lives and some may be more characteristic of certain stages of our development. The resolution of some conflicts may be only partial and their impact may be experienced from time to time, particularly when we are under stress. A good example of this, according to psychoanalytic theory, is that of the Oedipal conflict. It is believed that children (at least those in Western society) between the ages of 3–4 years develop a strong attachment to the parent of the opposite sex. This gives rise to feelings of rivalry towards the parent of the same sex, who in turn becomes a source of threat and retaliation. It is argued that these feelings of attraction, and the conflict associated with them, are never thoroughly resolved and we are likely to experience echoes of this early conflict throughout our lives as we forge new relationships. This may account for the fact that some of our relationships in adult life repeat the dynamics evident in our own family.

● **Departures from the Traditional Freudian Way**

To fashion a model of man reminiscent of the models which obtained in the physical sciences was obviously attractive to Freud, the natural scientist, but this approach was not so appealing to others. Indeed, theory development of this sort became a point of departure for some theorists including two associates of Freud, namely Carl G. Jung (1968) and Alfred Adler (1956). Each of them became disenchanted with Freud's biological emphasis and, in particular, with his emphasis on the sexual drive. Jung was more concerned to produce a theory which stressed the psychological aspects of man's development and functioning. He is perhaps best known for his interest in the underdeveloped aspects of the Ego and in the emergence of introversive and extraversive tendencies. Playing down the unconscious aspects of motivation, Adler took a more social view of man. He emphasized the importance of such influences as birth order, sibling rivalry, 'inferiority complex' (he invented the term) and the person's wish to 'be somebody'.

Modern theories have continued this drift away from the emphasis on the dynamic interplay among competing biological drives occurring within the individual. Successors to the early theorists argue that such notions, whilst not to be discounted entirely, are too simple and do not reflect the complexity and subtlety of human behaviour. Moreover, it might be argued that attempting to construe human behaviour in terms of 'forces', 'energies' and 'structures' sounds too much like a desperate but inappropriate effort to mimic the style of reasoning and theory development characteristic of the physical sciences.

An equally important fact, which has itself contributed to a revision of theory and practice, has been the nature of the problems and symptoms presented by patients. Commonly, therapists are confronted with patients whose major concerns are not clearly defined symptoms, such as those with which Freud dealt, but rather a general dissatisfaction with themselves as people and/or with their interpersonal relationships. Bowlby's work on 'attachment behaviour' (Bowlby, 1979), Mahler (1967) and the efforts of the Object Relations Theorists, such as Fairbairn (1952), Winnicott (1958) and Balint (1968), are important examples of theoretical developments which reflect (and at the same time help us to deal with) contemporary clinical problems. According to these theorists, the primary motivational drive in humans is to seek relationships with others and the difficulties or, indeed, the successes people have in relationships can usually be traced to the influence of very early relationships, particularly that between mother and child. In therapy, if we pursue this line of reasoning, we must focus not just on the individual patient's symptoms, or even on the patient as an individual, but rather on the patient in the context of this relationship with others. This approach is also consistent with Systems Theory and with the neo-Freudian schools of therapy, to which clinicians such as Horney (1939), Erikson (1950) and Sullivan (1955) contributed so much.

The work of Melanie Klein (Segal, 1964) also needs noting. It was largely developed in London. The main features include a placing-at-birth of the individual's affects and instincts and a literal acceptance of the death instinct which manifests as aggression and envy, the gradual working through of which hopefully leads to an integration of the personality, so that remnants of this death instinct become accommodated by reparation and sublimation.

Another group of theorists, referred to as the Ego Analysts, who include among their ranks Hartmann (1958) and Rapaport (1951), have also made a significant contribution to our understanding of human behaviour and experience, by directing our attention to the way in which man guides and is largely responsible for his own actions. Their emphasis on man's 'self determination' entailed an important shift in our view of man. He is not being portrayed as a hapless victim of irresistible and turbulent internal (intrapsychic) forces; instead, he is being depicted as the major architect in the construction of his own present and future.

Despite these and other more recent developments, strong traces of the more traditional Freudian notions reappear, sometimes under a different guise. To some extent, this is the case with aspects of Berne's theory of Transactional Analysis (Berne, 1966). One of the key concepts generated by this theory is that of 'Ego-states', of which Berne identified three: the 'Child', the 'Adult' and the 'Parent'. The boundaries of these Ego-states are not hard and fast but, according to Berne, at different times one of these states may assume control, giving our behaviour and experience a characteristic 'flavour'. The 'Parent' is similar to the more traditional idea of the Superego, in that it refers to that part of our personality which reflects the ideals and moral values of the family and culture to which we belong. The 'Child' makes its presence felt when, for instance, we 'let our hair down' and act on our more basic, egocentric and less socially acceptable impulses. Behaving in this way might also be described as allowing the Id to assume control. The remaining Ego-state, the 'Adult', is that part of ourselves which allows us to deal rationally and maturely with our own internal needs. Again, the correspondence can be seen between this concept and the more traditional Freudian one — the Ego.

Before we leave this topic, one particular point justifies repetition and that is the importance of conflict. Obviously, theories about the nature of man abound. Some emphasize the physical and biological aspects of man, while others focus on the interpersonal and social influences, but the theme which tends to link all these theories is that of the potential for and importance of conflict. Indeed, the contribution of conflict to man's diseases and dis-ease is a characteristic feature of psychodynamic theory.

- ### What are the Basic Aims of this Therapy?

One of the earliest forms of therapy for mental illness was catharsis, and this was used long before a humane approach towards the mentally ill was adopted. Catharsis (or, as it is sometimes called, 'abreaction') prevailed as a means of 'treatment' even when mental disorder was attributed to demoniacal possession. A cathartic experience can be defined as one in which there is an uninhibited and often dramatic expression of pent-up feelings, achieved by the relating and/or 'reliving' of significant past experiences, or sometimes by the acting-out of anticipated events or experiences. The alleged value of this is captured in such laymen's expressions as 'letting off steam', 'getting it off your chest' and 'getting it out of your system'.

In the absence of this emotional release, it was believed that the uncomfortable feelings would continue to build up emotional pressure until finally they would 'leak out' or, worse still, 'erupt' in some maladaptive way, such as through the development of mental and/or physical ill health. This view certainly has an intuitive appeal and no doubt catharsis does effect some relief, but the theory upon which the use of catharsis or abreaction is based may owe more to vulcanology than it does to psychology. It is not that giving vent to feelings has no value: the doubt is that it may offer only short term, symptomatic relief rather than long term improvement and durable change. One argument raised is that, in the absence of the patient understanding thoroughly why he behaves and feels the way he does, there will be only a short term remission of symptoms followed by a re-emergence of them or the development of new ones. This harks back to the notion of 'symptom-oriented' versus 'problem-oriented' treatment which arose in the consideration of the historical development of psychodynamic therapy.

Insight, or self-awareness, is not usually a quality with which most of us are over-endowed. Each person tends to build up his own private view of himself and of his world, and often this view turns out to be highly deceptive and inconsistent with the view held by others about him and his world. Sometimes the discrepancy may be quite innocuous, or humorous; but unfortunately it can also be the basis of a good deal of unhappiness and, worse still, illness. For example, if, for reasons which lie deep in his past, a patient were to see the world as a place full of threat, hostility and rejection, he might try to defend himself by withdrawing from human relationships, trusting nobody and rejecting others before they can reject him. This is hardly a formula for interpersonal success, and he would run the considerable risk of ending up feeling depressed, unloved, lonely and frustrated.

In his case, the aim of therapy would be to help him to understand the role of his previous, unhappy personal relationships in the development of this jaundiced view of life and of his symptoms. He would have to learn to accept, therefore, some responsibility for his feelings, for his view of the world and for his symptoms. This should be a learning process and not a confession. In the eyes of the doctor of a psychodynamic orientation, other treatment options such as medication, electroconvulsive therapy and many forms of behaviour therapy would be seen as inappropriate, on the grounds that they would be aiming at symptom relief, leaving the 'real' problem untouched. The argument about whether one should deal with symptoms of underlying causes is a long and complicated one. Frankly, I doubt if the supporters of either view could find sufficient and acceptable empirical evidence to achieve a full justification of their view.

Unfortunately, even the provision of insight and the opportunity for catharsis do not guarantee behavioural change. There are various motives which make it difficult to behave in different ways and to 'give up' symptoms, despite new insights. One reason is that changing our ways and presenting ourselves differently to the world, like any form of change, carries with it a risk that things might turn out to be even worse. It is sometimes a matter of the devil you know being rather safer than the one you do not know. For example, some patients fear that if they reveal their feelings or certain facets of their personalities, which previously they have hidden from themselves as well as from others, then there is a risk that other people will find them unacceptable and even less desirable than previously.

● Ego Defence Mechanisms

Another important aim of therapy, therefore, should be to help the patient adapt to changes in functioning and attitudes which therapy has brought about. The value of this aim is particularly evident when the patient is required to give up or modify certain coping strategies called *ego defence mechanisms*. These are particularly important concepts in psychodynamic theory and it will be valuable to consider them in some detail. To emphasize their dynamic and adaptive nature, it would probably be more appropriate to use the word 'processes' rather than the word 'mechanisms'. However, the latter — probably reflecting again the influence of the physical sciences — has gained such a secure foothold in the language of psychodynamics that it will continue to be used here.

The purpose of these defences is to protect us (or our Egos) from being disturbed or, worse, overwhelmed by our emotions — anxiety being the most obvious and common example. Anxiety may be created by external factors, such as separation, loss, illness and trauma, but it may also be created by internal ones, such as ideas, wishes, emotions and memories. The protection offered by these mechanisms comes from the fact that they enable us to distort, reject, transform or inhibit our awareness of feelings, ideas, sense impressions and other things which might threaten our self-esteem and composure. Generally, these defences operate at an unconscious level so that we are unaware of what it is that evokes the defence. They should not be regarded, therefore, as conscious attempts to lie or deceive.

Many defence mechanisms have been described in the clinical and theoretical literature, but it will be sufficient to explore four examples which will help us to see how these defences enable us to cope with reality.

Repression

This is the process whereby disturbing ideas, memories or feelings, which threaten to become conscious, are retained or relegated to an unconscious level. A good example of repression was provided by a patient of mine who, as a child, suffered very serious burns to the throat and neck because of carelessness on the part of her mother. Ten years have passed and the patient is still quite unable to recall anything about the incident or its sequelae, requiring intravenous feeding and extensive skin grafting. The family have never discussed with the patient what actually happened, instead, it is as though the accident had never happened. Interestingly, her presenting symptom was an inability to swallow food in public places because, as she said, 'It sticks in my throat'.

To refer to her problem of recall as 'mere forgetfulness' would be to ignore the fact that to recollect the incident and describe it would necessitate her being reminded of the full horror, pain, distress and anger associated with the episode. It is not difficult, therefore, to understand why this girl had 'blocked off' this dreadful incident in her life.

Projection

Another means of dealing with uncomfortable emotions or attitudes is to resist acknowledging them within oneself and to attribute them to others. This is called projection. For example, if a person found it difficult to accept his own capacity to be hostile and rejecting, one way to resolve this would be to 'project' (unconsciously) these characteristics on to others, allowing him thereby to accuse them of being angry and rejecting towards him. An extreme form of this process can be seen in patients who suffer from a disorder called paranoia. A paranoid patient is characteristically hypersensitive to what he considers to be humiliation or rebuffs. By means of projection, he tends to distort his perception of what would have been entirely innocuous or friendly actions and comments by others and views them as challenging and hostile. His belief that the world is an aggressive and threatening place then appears to provide the paranoid patient with justification for taking retaliatory action. Because the patient sees himself as only reacting to the aggressiveness of others, his own anger and even violence will then seem entirely justifiable to him and no longer threatening to his own self-image.

Displacement

Scapegoating is a well-known method of ridding oneself of frustration and anger. In psychodynamic terms, this is referred to as displacement. For instance, if a doctor were extremely angry with one of his patients, but felt unable to express this feeling directly to the patient, one way to deal with this uncomfortable, pent-up emotion would be to redirect it towards his secretary. He might complain, for instance, about some minor error or indiscretion which under other circumstances would have evoked no response from him. This redirection of his anger would make him feel better for two related reasons. Firstly, he would have managed to rid himself of his anger and, secondly, he would have been able to do so in a way which did not threaten his own view of himself, which does not include being angry with patients.

Denial

Denial is another form of defence against anxiety and it refers to the inability of the individual to acknowledge some reality. Commonly, it is displayed by relatives who have just been informed of the sudden and unexpected death of a loved one: 'Oh, he can't be dead!' is a characteristic response. It may also be seen in people who have a serious or life-threatening illness and yet refuse to recognise the significance of their symptoms, and avoid seeking the appropriate help, despite apparently incontrovertible and substantial evidence to support the diagnosis. One might also consider that the family of the badly burned patient, referred to earlier, were displaying denial by behaving as though the accident had never occurred.

Somatization

In a textbook such as this, somatization must be included among the mechanisms of defence. Even today it is more acceptable to one's *amour propre* to present to a doctor with, say, asthma, migraine, indigestion or hypertension than with recurrent anxiety states, depressions or, worse, psychotic breakdowns.

Before we move on from the topic of Ego defence mechanisms, three points should be underlined and noted. The first is that we all use such defences — it is not just patients who do so — because they can be adaptive by providing a means of coping, if only temporarily, with events or feelings which otherwise would be too disturbing and disruptive. It is when the defences themselves prove too 'costly' for the individual (in mental or physical terms), or to his environment in terms of antisocial behaviour, i.e. when the defences break down, that doctors or the judiciary may be called in. Medical students are often faced with anxiety-provoking situations which threaten their composure (Alexander and Haldane, 1979, 1980). For example, their first experiences at the dissecting table can be very distressing and, as a consequence, a variety of defences are marshalled to protect them from this anxiety. As a temporary device, for example, denial of feelings may be a convenient protective shield through which reality can percolate at a rate at which the individual can adjust and adapt (*see* Chap. 3, p. 33). It is only when such defences are used excessively and become more a way of life that, far from being adaptive and constructive, they can have a constricting and crippling effect on the development of our personality. This is the case with certain neurotic illnesses and personality disorders. Similarly, a problem can arise when the doctor's own emotional defences against anxiety block his perception and understanding of his patient's emotional problems. This may occur, for example, when the doctor's response to anxiety and discomfiture is to distance himself from his patient by being 'cool' and 'objective'. Such a reaction may give the patient the message that emotional expressions are unacceptable. Thus, general practitioners will gradually acquire a 'list' of patients with whom they can be mutually comfortable.

The second point is that insensitive assaults in therapy on these defences are not only likely to be unproductive therapeutically, but may even be damaging to the patient. Unfortunately, for some doctors the glimpse of a defence mechanism displayed by patients seems to arouse a missionary zeal, a *furor therapeuticus*, which inspires them to demolish the defence and try to 'deal with' the underlying anxiety. It is a bit like kicking a crutch away from a man with a broken leg and then looking puzzled, if not aggrieved, because he falls down in pain rather than offering his profuse thanks. The defences must be respected. A more therapeutic aim would be to help the patient to use his defence in a flexible and constructive way. Moreover, if the patient can be helped to identify what it is that he needs to be defended from, then other more adaptive and constructive means of dealing with the threat might be found.

The third and final point is that the protection offered by such defences is rarely foolproof. Powerful conflicts and feelings have a tendency to 'leak out' into consciousness, and may present themselves at the most inappropriate time and in the most inappropriate way. One doctor became acutely aware of this at the end of a supervision session, in which she had been confronted by me about her tendency to 'forget' what I had repeatedly told her. She stated, 'It's not that I try to remember, eh, I mean to forget what you tell me.'!

●   What are the Characteristic Features of the Therapeutic Relationship?

1.   The 'contract'

Despite the variety of theories embraced by the psychodynamic model, there does seem to be a consensus about the crucial role of the relationship between the doctor and the patient. First and foremost, it is a *professional* relationship, however caring and dedicated the clinician. Because of this, there are limits to what may take place between him and his patient: it is a case of disciplined intimacy. To some extent the limits are determined by the aims of therapy, because the purpose of the relationship is to foster and facilitate activities and conditions which are therapeutic or potentially therapeutic.

As in other potential relationships, there should be a mutually agreed 'contract' between the two parties. In other words, the doctor and the patient should each be aware of what it is they are seeking to do and how they are going to achieve this. Not only does the establishment of a 'contract' help to ensure that their work together is purposeful, but the process of defining the goals can be helpful to the patient. If you cannot explain to your patient what you are going to do and how it might help him, you should not start treatment. Patients often come feeling so overwhelmed by their symptoms and problems that helping them to define and identify what has to be done, and why, is itself an important and reassuring step in the treatment. The restoration of hope and clarity is no mean achievement.

2.   Transference and countertransference

One of Freud's earliest observations was that, in the course of therapy, patients developed strong emotions towards him. These reactions Freud assumed were unrealistic and were related to the patients' experiences in earlier relationships, particularly those with their parents. 'Transference' was the technical term he introduced to describe this tendency of patients to direct to him feelings and attitudes which would have been more appropriately directed to other significant persons in their lives. At first, transference was regarded as a barrier to treatment, but Freud soon realised that understanding the transference reaction was a valuable way of gaining insight into how a patient distorted his view of himself and of others. Thereafter, many therapists saw the understanding and analysis of the transference as the major focus of psychoanalytic therapy.

Transference feelings may be positive or negative and often there is a mixture of both. Positive transference can be seen in the way the patient describes his doctor, for example, in unrealistically glowing terms, and also in the way he tries to translate the professional relationship into a social and personal one.

'Chance' meetings carefully contrived by the patient, or suggestions to extend the number of appointments, may indicate the patient's positive transference. Negative transference may be shown by expressions of hostility and rejection, or by failing to keep appointments, or persistent unpunctuality, or requests for a second opinion.

The therapeutic relationship can, therefore, be seen as a microcosm of the patient's world of interpersonal relationships, past, present and future. It provides an opportunity for the close and systematic analysis of how the patient behaves in relationship, his expectations, his needs and his defences. In addition, the therapeutic relationship serves as a testing-ground, or an interpersonal 'laboratory', in which the patient can explore and experiment with other ways of coping in relationships. For example, the patient may learn to express better his anger and other feelings which he has feared ventilating in the past. It is for this reason that this form of therapy has been described as an exercise in 'reparenting'. There is, however, nothing intrinsically therapeutic in the occurrence of transference: the crucial factor is the way in which transference feelings are dealt with in therapy. It is likely that transference occurs to a degree in all relationships, but it is easy to see why it is more likely to occur where there is ambiguity and an opportunity for misinterpretation in a relationship. Although the rather passive and enigmatic figure of the psychotherapist is a rich vein of humour for cartoonists and satirists, this 'masterly inactivity' is not a mere façade but a purposeful tactic. By deliberately limiting the extent to which his own feelings and values intrude in the therapeutic relationship, and by reflecting back to the patient those feelings and values he has 'transferred' to the therapeutic relationship, the doctor has an excellent means of helping the patient to understand how he perceives (or misperceives) himself and his relationship with others. Obviously, it would be unrealistic to imagine that any doctor could present himself as a completely 'blank screen'. Each therapeutic relationship is unique and each will evoke some of the doctor's own characteristics and qualities, but the aim is to minimize the extent to which these interfere with the emergence of transference.

A corollary to this description of the stance to be adopted by the doctor is that he must resist the temptation to satisfy the patient's neurotic needs, especially those for love and affection. This can be difficult. It is not comfortable being seen by patients as unloving, uncaring and rejecting, when one is dedicated to helping them. Sometimes, the temptation is very strong to 'correct' the patient's misinterpretation of what one is trying to do and of what sort of person one is. It is also possible to 'prove' to the patient that one cares by creating a highly dependent relationship in which the patient feels secure and shielded from all responsibilities. Although it perhaps offers temporary respite for the patient, this solves nothing in the long run, because the doctor has colluded in recreating in therapy the type of relationship in which the patient usually becomes trapped and which usually turns out to be self-defeating and unsatisfying. The doctor has behaved a bit like the parent who never allows the child to grow up and tries to satisfy every infantile need 'in order to keep him happy'.

As in the case with all therapeutic tools, the therapeutic relationship can be put to bad as well as good use. For instance, the relationship does provide the clinician with an opportunity of being punitive and hostile to his patient under the apparently respectable guise of a therapeutic tactic. Alternatively, the neurotic dependence and flattery of the patient may not be recognised for what they are, and the doctor may unhelpfully and unthinkingly exploit them. A doctor who constantly needs to be flattered and rewarded by his patients is likely to become the victim of this need to be gratified. It is more helpful if the doctor tries to understand what lies behind the patient's incessant need to please him. There are many possible motives — these include seducing the doctor into trying to solve the patient's problems, frustrating therapy and distracting the doctor from his principal task.

This issue of the doctor's feelings towards the patient introduces another important concept — countertransference. In the same way that patients bring their past interpersonal experiences into the therapeutic relationship, doctors may also tend to react to their patients in terms of their own experiences in previous relationships: this tendency is known as 'countertransference'. As with transference, countertransference may be positive or negative. Psychotherapists may display negative countertransference by subtly (or sometimes not so subtly!) denigrating their patients by making impossible or conflicting demands on them, or by 'forgetting' what patients had said the previous week. Positive countertransference may be revealed in various ways, including offering additional sessions or extending the sessions well beyond the allocated time. There was the case of one particular colleague of mine who even said 'Thank you' to his patient at the end of the therapy sessions! Once he became aware of his own unconscious feelings, however, he was able to use countertransference as a barometer of what was going on in therapy. In this way, countertransference can serve as a useful function: it is not something we need fear and disclaim. It may be helpful on occasions to share your own feelings with the patient. A doctor's saying, 'I'm feeling a bit confused by this and I'm not sure where we should go from here — maybe that's the way you're feeling too' is not an unprofessional admission of incompetence. *On the contrary, it conveys an empathic understanding* of the patient's feelings and indicates the honesty of the doctor as well as his willingness to continue to face the patient's problems.

The potential influence of countertransference demands, therefore, a good deal of basic self-awareness and a willingness to scrutinize our own behaviour and feelings in our relationships with patients. It is in recognition of this need that some authorities advocate that the doctor who wishes to practise dynamic psychotherapy should undergo a training analysis, or at least some form of personal therapeutic experience. Certainly, the significance of countertransference makes the need for supervision of therapy very obvious. Didactic teaching and reading can only give us a superficial awareness of the issues involved.

While most clinicians would acknowledge the ubiquity and general importance of transference and countertransference, these terms have unfortunately been the subject of many definitions which have resulted in confusion rather than clarity. For example, one extreme view, espoused by the Kleinian school of therapy, is that *all* the interactions between doctor and patient are a product of transference and countertransference. Apart from the fact that this is not a testable propositon, if so much is attributed to these concepts they appear to explain so much and yet they explain nothing. According to that proposition, all behaviour and experiences would merely be a replay of earlier patterns of behaviour and experience. It is probably more helpful, therefore, to restrict the use of 'transference' to refer to those *inappropriate* feelings and attitudes which the patient develops towards the doctor *in the course of therapy*, because he distorts his image of the doctor in the light of his earlier experiences in important relationships. (The patient is firmly convinced, of course, that his own reactions are entirely appropriate to the circumstance.) Countertransference can then be viewed as the complement to the patient's transference. If, as their relationship developed, a patient were to begin responding to the doctor in a childlike and dependent way as though the doctor were a parent, then this would be interpreted as transference. If, in response to this form of behaviour from the patient, the doctor began treating him as though he was a dependent child, then this would be a case of countertransference. (According to Berne's theory, this would be a 'Parent-Child' relationship.) The use of these more restricted definitions allows us to acknowledge the occurrence of non-transference and non-countertransference reactions between the therapist and the patient. We must not forget that there are two real people engaged in a real relationship.

3.   The therapeutic alliance

More recently, increased attention has been given to another element in the therapeutic relationship and that is what is called the 'therapeutic alliance'. Freud and the early analysts were aware of the importance of this feature, but they regarded it as another aspect of transference. Perhaps it is easier to consider that there are two 'parts' of the patient. The first 'part' is sick, unhappy and yet resistant to change, whereas the other 'part' is hopeful, co-operative and willing to change. It is with the second 'part' of the patient that the doctor has to ally himself. In Berne's terminology, the therapeutic alliance is an 'Adult-Adult' relationship in which the two participants agree to co-operate, at a mature and adult level, to achieve the goals of therapy. In this way, the patient becomes an active agent in his own treatment, rather than behaving as a passive recipient of the clinician's skills and care. This is not the same, however, as describing the patient as being 'well-motivated' for therapy: many patients are keen to 'get better', but their expectations may be quite unrealistic and based on the assumption that the improvement in their health or circumstances is solely the responsibility of the doctor. (Of course, one should not blame patients for this expectation, because it is what they have been taught to expect from a traditional doctor-patient relationship). As part of the therapeutic alliance the patient must achieve a realistic view of what the doctor can and should offer, and become aware of the extent to which a successful outcome will depend on his own efforts to help himself. The patient must also be willing to tolerate periods of frustration, disillusionment and emotional discomfort. Unfortunately, this is too much for some patients and they take what is described as a 'flight into health', reporting after only a few interviews that they are 'cured' and leave, expressing profuse gratitude to their very talented and kindly doctor! Achieving a therapeutic alliance is probably easier if the doctor and the patient like each other, but this is not essential. Mutual trust and respect are probably more important: they have to be earned.

This section would not be complete if the issue of terminating therapy were not mentioned. The end of the therapeutic relationship is an event of signal importance, particularly if the relationship has been of some months' duration, as is frequently the case. Indeed, it is in recognition of its importance that it is generally argued that termination should be built into the plans for therapy. Under ideal circumstances, one would like the end of therapy to be the natural outcome of the achievements of the therapeutic goals. Unfortunately, this is frequently not the reason for therapy ending. Many factors conspire to produce a premature terminaton: these include the waning motivation of the patient, the departure from the region of the patient or the doctor and significant changes in the patient's circumstances. However, while accepting that many terminations are not 'ideal', the clinician should always consider, when formulating with the patient the goals of therapy, what criteria would be used to decide when therapy should be terminated.

● **What are the Techniques and Skills associated with this Therapy?**

One of Freud's patients aptly described psychoanalysis as the 'talking cure' and, from the time Freud stopped using hypnosis, the bedrock of the psychodynamic therapies has been the verbal interchange between the patient and the doctor. Non-verbal behaviour is certainly important as a dimension of communication, but even this usually has to be dealt with verbally at some stage. Most of the talking is done by the patient, particularly if the psychotherapist is encouraging the use of free association. Despite the trusting and facilitating atmosphere and relationship, talking in this uninhibited way can be arduous and stressful for the patient and he will often show signs of a reluctance to continue. A similar reluctance may be shown by the patient to grasp what the doctor has suggested or to stick to the therapeutic contract. 'Resistance' is the technical term used to describe such efforts of the patient to maintain the status quo and to avoid proceeding with therapy. It is not at all helpful merely to criticise or disparage the patient because he shows signs of resistance. Nor should these signs of resistance be taken as confirmation that the patient does not want to help. Instead, the doctor should try to understand, and help the patient to understand, the source of the anxiety which lies behind the resistance. Most of us find it difficult to reveal very personal material, however trustworthy and receptive the audience, but, from the point of view of therapy, it is very often those things which the patient fears to disclose that provide the essential material for therapy.

We are not, however, powerless in the face of patients' resistance. We can make use of four techniques — confrontation, clarification, interpretation and 'working through'. These are the basic tools of psychodynamic therapy to be used to facilitate communication, to enhance understanding, to encourage the expression of feelings and to foster durable change.

'Confrontation', as the name suggests, means directing the patient's attention to something that he has done, said or experienced, but of which his awareness of having done it, or at least his awareness of its significance, is minimal. This technique should not be seen to be a justification for bullying or being rude to patients.

Another technique for increasing the patient's awareness is that of 'clarification' — that is to say, teasing out the relevant from the irrelevant features of the material presented by the patient. This may be done by rephrasing or reflecting back to the patient what he has said, or by skilfully questioning around a particular theme or issue.

'Interpretation' is a rather more complicated technique and one which has become a source of conflicting opinion. In brief, it refers to that process whereby the doctor *offers* the patient a new perspective on or new meaning of something the patient has presented, perhaps in the form of dreams, symptoms, feelings and behaviour. The doctor has to avoid, therefore, taking too much at face value. Rather, he examines material as it is presented (the 'manifest content') in an effort to find some underlying meaning (the 'latent content'). Sometimes in his interpretations he will try to link together what otherwise seem to the patient to be unrelated and discontinuous ideas, feelings and events. This may be achieved, for instance, by helping the patient to integrate what goes on in therapy with what has happened in the past or what is happening in the present. The frequent focus on past events is not merely an empty biographical exercise. In a sense, the past is ever present because it continues to have an effect on how we structure our lives. We ought to be aware of this effect because, as Santayana, the American philosopher, has warned, 'Those who do not remember the past are condemned to relive it'; they 'act it out'. The past should not be a straitjacket and therefore many patients have been freed from it.

Learning when, what and how to make interpretations is a skill not easily acquired and students of psychotherapy often react in two entirely different ways. Some, impressed by the powerful effect of interpretation, strafe their patients with interpretations; but, as one might expect, poorly timed and insensitive interpreting is likely only to jeopardize the therapeutic relationship, leaving patients more disturbed, hurt and confused than they were before therapy began. At the other extreme, some are too reluctant to interpret because they are not sure that the interpretation is 'correct'. This, however, is the wrong way to look at interpretations. The reality is that no therapist has been granted a gift of infallible observation and judgement, and therefore an interpretation has the status only of a hypothesis to be tested. Suggestions such as 'I wonder if you aren't feeling rather angry and fed up just now' are usually more appropriate than are bold statements such as 'You're feeling angry and fed up'. The doctor has to listen for themes and echoes and offer an interpretation to the patient as an alternative way of making sense of his behaviour and experience. This requires psychotherapists to be able to tolerate ambiguity and uncertainty just as their patients have to do.

'Working through' is an equally important concept, although it has become a cliché. Correctly used, it applies to the inevitably time-consuming process of exploring and digesting new ideas, experiences and insights. To 'see ourselves as others see us', or to change our view of the world and to test out new ways of behaving are not easy tasks because we need time to consolidate, monitor and adjust to these changes and their consequences, including the reactions of others. One particular change to which a patient may have to adapt is the loss of his symptoms. Not only do some symptoms provide the patient with 'primary gain' (by protecting him from emotional discomfort), but they may also achieve 'secondary gain' either by evoking the sympathy and attention of other people, or by giving the patient a means of controlling his environment. It is not difficult to imagine, for example, how certain symptoms, such as headaches, frigidity and depression may create secondary gain for the patient. It is frequently the threatened loss of secondary gain that accounts for the resilience of symptoms despite heroic treatment efforts. Some patients do not enjoy good health!

There are two additional points to be noted. The first is that no matter how important the therapy is to the patient, the 'treatment hour' is but one twenty-fourth of the patient's day. Neither the patient nor the doctor can afford to ignore the realities of the patient's life, for the ultimate test of change and development is not how the patient fares in therapy, but how he deals with these realities. The second point is that no matter how skilled the doctor is in the use of the techniques and methods just described, he will make no progress unless he listens empathically to his patient. It is a pity that the capacity to listen is often undervalued among clinicians and students. Too much emphasis can be placed on doing something to or for patients. This may be one reason why, in the early stages of their training in psychodynamic therapy, doctors tend to ask too many questions, instead of adopting a rather more passive, listening role.

● **What Problems or Patients can be Best Helped by this Therapy**

Now that we have covered some features of the theory, aims, methods and techniques of psychodynamic therapy, it will already be obvious that this form of therapy is not suitable for all patients. It is for this reason that the general question, 'Does it work?' is a ridiculous one. If anybody asked, 'Do throat lozenges work?', one would not be able to give an unqualified answer. They may be helpful for certain throat ailments, but they are not too useful if you happen to have venereal disease!

We need to be more specific about what therapy, carried out by whom, under what conditions, works for which patients with what problems. Although research has not generated very specific findings, we do have some guidelines (eg. Bloch, 1979).

First of all, with this form of therapy, little progress is likely to be made with patients who are in the grip of one of the most serious and incapacitating forms of mental illness, called psychosis. Psychotic patients are so out of contact with reality that they find it almost impossible to engage in a realistic way with a psychotherapist. Secondly, patients of very limited intelligence and verbal fluency are not going to gain much from a therapy which is so evidently biased towards reasoning, understanding and verbal communication. (It is important, however, not to exaggerate such factors. Even patients of limited intelligence can be suitable for this therapy providing the doctor makes sufficient effort to explain things and work at a level consistent with the patient's abilities and experience.) Thirdly, although this is not a problem exclusive to psychodynamic therapy, patients who either have no real motivation to change or have grossly unrealistic expectations of therapy are not good prospects. Some patients are quite refractory to insight, and others see doctors as merchants of happiness who will provide them with a 'cure' and contentment without any effort on their own part. Fourthly, the doctor has a responsibility to ensure that the patients' personal, social and family resources would allow them to cope with the demands of therapy. Finally, patients who find it difficult to think in psychological terms, are not at all introspective and are not able to reflect candidly on themselves, are likely to find this form of therapy unrewarding and unnecessarily stressful.

As one gains more experience in using this form of treatment, one often finds that more patients than one had expected turn out to be suitable. In any case, even if these guidelines are employed quite strictly, there is no shortage of patients to be helped. Patients with problems in relationships, neurotic disorders, grief reactions or disorders of personality as well as those with psychosomatic disorders can be regarded as possible candidates for psychodynamic therapy. (With regard to the last group, it is revealing to note that anything between 30%–40% of patients present to their family doctors with physical symptoms which have no detectable organic cause.)

In deciding for or against the use of psychodynamic therapy, one should avoid being unduly influenced by the patient's clinical problem or diagnosis. Two patients with the same clinical picture will have their own constellation of relationships, their own personal view of life and their own attitudes to therapy and change. Moreover, helping patients in a dyadic relationship is but one way of using psychodynamic principles and techniques. For historical reasons, and for clarity of presentation, individual psychotherapy has been the focus of our attention, but these principles and techniques can also be used in working with couples, families and groups.

• Summary and Conclusions

As a means of alleviating a patient's distress, the distinctive feature of psychodynamic therapy is its focus on unconscious mental processes and events which are thought to underlie the patient's symptom or presenting problem. The therapeutic relationship is regarded as the critical element in therapy because it is in the context of this safe, caring but *professional* relationship that the patient can become aware of and explore the significance of this unconscious material.

The assumptions that this form of therapy makes about man and his ills do not, however, deny the importance of other influences such as genetics, the environment and culture. It is also important to be aware that this mainly verbal form of therapy is not necessarily incompatible with other forms of treatment, such as medication or behaviour therapy, provided that there is a sound therapeutic rationale to the concurrent use of other forms of help. For instance, it is quite possible that a very depressed patient might require a course of antidepressants in order that he can function at a level whereby he could benefit from psychotherapy.

Classical psychoanalysis is undoubtedly the prototype of the numerous varieties of psychodynamic therapy which have emerged. Some of these modifications have developed from the prototype, whereas others have probably appeared as a reaction against the original model. Sociocultural factors have probably played a part as well in the shaping of new therapeutic approaches. For instance, Western society has changed, since the early days of psychoanalysis, from being highly authoritarian and rigidly hierarchical to being more democratic and egalitarian. Part of this change may be reflected in the therapeutic relationship which has developed from a benign but distant 'father-child' relationship into a more open and flexible one. Another important change is that psychodynamic therapy is not used solely, as it was initially, to treat mental illness and relieve symptoms; instead it is often used to help people with 'problems of living'. The boundary between 'treatment' and 'personal growth' has now become extremely blurred.

To judge from its increasing popularity, it is obvious that psychodynamic therapy is a 'growth industry' but, regrettably, the evaluation of this form of therapy remains a 'cottage industry'. Perhaps the general issue of its effectiveness is no longer in doubt (Garfield and Bergin, 1978), but we still remain in relative ignorance about what are the effective elements in the process of therapy: more research is clearly required. However, just because we do not have as yet incontrovertible empirical support for our theories and techniques we must not disband them in despair. They are a genuine attempt to structure and make sense of what practitioners do and how patients respond. Until more data are available, each practitioner will have to act as his own 'researcher', looking candidly at his results and examining the assumptions which underlie his work. This will also require him to consider how to blend professional skills and knowledge together with his personal qualities and his wish to care for his patient. Being merely 'caring' and 'compassionate' is not enough (and, in any case, practitioners of psychotherapy have no monopoly of such qualities). Nonetheless, doctors must not let the technical aspects of the treatment stand in the way of what must be their primary task — the alleviation of suffering. Faced with difficult clinical situations it can be tempting for the doctor to hide behind techniques, jargon and theories. Facile intellectualizations about the patient suffering from 'an unresolved Oedipal conflict' may provide the insecure therapist with a spurious sense of understanding of his patient's problem, but such statements guarantee no relief of suffering for the patient.

References and Further Reading

Adler A. (1956) *The Individual Psychology of Alfred Adler*. Basic Books, New York.
Alexander D.A. and Haldane J.D.H. (1979) Medical education: a student perspective. *Medical Education,* **13**, 336–41.
Alexander D.A. and Haldane J.D.H. (1980) Medical education: the discontinuers' view. *Medical Education* **14**, 16–22.
Balint M. (1968) *The Basic Fault*. Tavistock Publications, London.
Bellack L. (1981) *Crises and Special Problems in Psychoanalysis and Psychotherapy*. Brunner/Mazel, New York.
Berne E. (1966) *Games People Play*. Deutsch, London.
Bloch S. (1979) *Assessment of Patients for Psychotherapy*. Brit. J. Psychiat. **135**, 193–208.
Bowlby J. (1979) *The Making and Breaking of Affectional Bonds*. Tavistock Publications, London.
Brown J.A.C. (1961) *Freud and the Post-Freudians*. Penguin, Harmondsworth.
Clark R.W. (1980) *Freud: The Man and the Cause*. Weidenfeld and Nicolson, London.
Dicks H.V. (1967) *Marital Tensions: Clinical Studies Towards a Psychological Theory of Interaction*. Routledge and Kegan Paul, London.
Ellenberger H.F. (1970) *The Discovery of the Unconscious*. Allen Lane, London.
Erikson E.H. (1950) *Childhood and Society*. Norton, New York.
Fairbairn W.R.D. (1952) *Psychoanalytic Studies of the Personality*. Routledge and Kegan Paul, London.
Foulkes S.H. and Anthony E.J. (1973) *Group Psychotherapy: The Psychoanalytic Approach*. Penguin, Harmondsworth.

Frank J.D. (1969) *Persuasion and Healing*. Schocken Books, New York.

Freud A. (1946) *The Ego and Mechanisms of Defence*. Hogarth, London.

Freud S. (1964) *An Outline of Psycho-Analysis*. Standard Edition Collected Works, Hogarth, London.

Garfield S.L. and Bergin A.E. (1978) *Handbook of Psychotherapy and Behavior Change* (Second Edition). Wiley, New York.

Garfield S.L. (1980) *Psychotherapy: An Eclectic Approach*. Wiley — Interscience, Chichester.

Glover E. (1955) *The Technique of Psychoanalysis*. International University Press, New York.

Guntrip H. (1977) *Psychoanalytic Theory, Therapy and Self*. Hogarth, London.

Hartmann H. (1958) *Ego Psychology and the Problem of Adaptation*. International Universities Press, New York.

Horney K. (1939) *New Ways in Psychoanalysis*. Norton, New York.

Jung C.G. (1968) *Analytical Pyschology: Its Theory and Practice*. Routledge and Kegan Paul, London.

Kovel J. (1978) *A Complete Guide to Therapy*. Pelican, Harmondsworth.

Mahler M. (1967) On Human Symbiosis and the Vicissitudes of Individualism. *J. Am. Psychoanal. Assn.*, **15**, 740–763.

Malan D. (1979) *Individual Psychotherapy and the Science of Psychodynamics*. Butterworths, Kent.

Rapaport D. (1951) *The Organization and Pathology of Thought*. Columbia University Press, New York.

Rychlak J.F. (1973) *Introduction to Personality and Psychotherapy: A Theory-Construction Approach*. Houghton Mifflin Co., Boston.

Segal H. (1964) *An Introduction to the Work of Melanie Klein*. Heinemann, London.

Storr A. (1979) *The Art of Psychotherapy*. Secker and Warburg and William Heinemann Medical, London.

Sullivan H.S. (1955) *The Interpersonal Theory of Psychiatry*. Tavistock Publications, London.

Sutherland S. (1976) *Breakdown*. Weidenfeld and Nicolson, London.

Szasz T. (1979) *The Myth of Psychotherapy*. Oxford University Press, Oxford.

Winnicott D.W. (1958) *Collected Papers*. Tavistock Publications, London.

3

The medical student's feelings and the clinical relationship

by Jon Sklar

It is difficult to imagine a comprehensive medical training that does not include elements of the significance of mental factors in illness and its treatment. Yet such shortcomings in medical education may later result in the blindness of physicians not interested in the problems of human living, both healthy and diseased. It may also lead to the training of practitioners who are less than skilful in their handling of the doctor-patient relationship and of the process of healing.

In contemporary medical training there are usually courses on medical psychology, which often take place early in the curriculum and, when such teaching is based on academic or experimental psychology preoccupied with the measurement of detail, it cannot meet the requirements of students wishing to understand the doctor-patient relationship.

The problem for both doctors and patients is that being human beings they have, inevitably, a range and depth of emotions and feelings. This is often particularly charged in relation to the body and body-illness. People have emotions about the ill parts of their body, which constitute at base a phantasy of the pathology. Knowing the truth usually helps to allay the fears regarding this phantasy. Of course, doctors themselves suffer from phantasies and medical students especially so. It is well known that the latter harbour at some time or another all the medical afflictions of their textbooks.

One vital aspect of *examining* patients is that emotions may be taken into account. They can be very involved and the doctor is often provoked to experience a whole range of feelings about the person he is invited to treat — these feelings include anger, common sympathy, caringness and antipathy. If the doctor is aware of them, they are much less likely to interfere with the communications with his patients, than if they remain unconscious.

The preoccupations of life may be said to be basically threefold: birth, sexuality and death, and these three preoccupy the 'internal world' of the human being, especially the world of a growing infant. The medical student has often a great burden to bear during his or her studies; somehow, all that must be learnt about bodies — nakedness, genitalia, sexuality, birth and death — has to be integrated into the student's own perception.

What, for instance, is the emotional impact of one young person examining another young person's body? On the surface, this seems an irrelevant question and it is usually ignored in medical school. Yet the trainee enters medical school with various notions and phantasies about bodies, theirs and other people's. To the student preoccupied with keeping 'hands to oneself', the idea of touching another's naked body may be a source of acute embarrassment, almost as if it were a sexual advance. Somehow the student has to stumble through all the 'sexuality' of the meeting of the doctor and patient, in a state of mind which is usually unprepared and in an atmosphere where such aspects of medical training are vigorously ignored.

I remember witnessing the mixture of horror and excitement in a male colleague who during training was asked to examine a young man. The latter shook and reacted as if having orgasm as the student attempted to palpate the abdomen. The patient was deeply embarrassed by his discharge soiling the sheets and the student likewise did not finish the examination, let alone the clerking. Similarly, how many students can cope with the demands made by the necessity to examine the body of a patient as old as that of one's parents? It may be extremely hard at first for the student to bear to look at 'parents'' nakedness.

What is the trainee to do in such a bewildering 'sexual' world? The underlying theme of medical education is to harden the student's attitude. This is the right and proper direction. Who would want to be treated by a surgeon who had qualms about sticking a knife into another person's body or by a doctor who fainted at the sight of blood and mess? It is likely that the beginning of such a toughening up of the character armour begins in the dissecting room where medical education has usually commenced. This fact, in itself, is an indictment of medical education, where the process of making a doctor begins with an experience of a dead body rather than the birth of a baby.

Yet this desirable process of defending himself against anxieties may become so exaggerated that the student builds such a tough armour around himself that feelings never come to be acknowledged and the future doctor may then be left untouched by death and pain.

If this splitting process develops too far, it can become a pathological state. The adolescent patient in casualty who swallows two aspirins more than the proper dose, with the expectation of death, may be perceived by the hardened doctor as not worthy of his medical expertise. It is not a medical emergency in which a life can be saved and the patient is whisked out of casualty by the doctor, who is angry at having his time wasted. And yet for that patient, the experience of being close to death may have been very high and it has gone quite unnoticed by the closed mind of the doctor, interested only in the body and distanced from the pain in the patient's mental state.

How else may medical students cope with such assaults on their emotions? The common occurrence of both heavy drinking and excessive sexuality in an often closed hospital/institutional system may be considered as defences against the anxieties on the part of trainees and trainers in the course of medical education. Instead of pondering on themes such as, 'One day, will I be old and have such and such an awful pain?', anxiety is relieved by dissolving it in alcohol or the forgetfulness that goes with coitus.

Up to a point, this is the stuff of an undergraduate life, with its crises of maturation. Yet medical students devolve into doctors, many of whom retain these apparent coping mechanisms which can in extreme cases be taken to the excesses of alcoholism, drug addiction and ultimately suicide. It may be argued that such issues have little to do with medicine, but I think the seeds may well be laid down in undergraduate training for such pathological splitting processes to occur in later life.

One method of investigating the anxieties and feelings of the medical student in relation to the beginnings of his clinical work is within the context of the training seminar. The difficulty is that such doctor-patient skills cannot be taught: they can only be experienced. Such a seminar is a development of Michael Balint's studies with general practitioners which in turn followed seminars with social workers dealing with marital difficulties. It became clear to Balint that ordinary didactic methods were of limited value, but if in the case discussion attention was focussed on the development of the client-worker relationship, a considerable increase in the worker's understanding and effectiveness resulted.

Extrapolation to a medical student group, where clinical problems are brought, in which the student feels stuck and lost, can be equally illuminating. The seminar is concerned with the understanding of the student-patient relationship. The aim of the seminar is to develop in the student a sensitivity to the patients' emotional problems to enable the former to understand them more precisely and in greater depth, and thereby to help him acquire skills and understanding for a greater therapeutic effect. To quote Balint, 'A pre-condition for the acquisition of this increased sensitivity is a general loosening up of the doctor's personality, especially with regard to his professional work. He must be able to notice and to tolerate emotional factors active in his patients that he rejected or ignored before and he must learn to accept them as worthy of his attention.'

Balint is discussing qualified doctors who have already acquired this professional armour. It is likely that medical students can benefit, by being invited not to don such protective measures so early in their training. The seminar technically compares a given individual's way of treating patients with those of his colleagues in the seminar. A group setting is used to demonstrate that any form of treatment entails a specific kind of interaction between the patient and the student doctor.

The realization may dawn on the seminar, including its leader, that mistakes may be made. The discovery that *the* correct therapy for any given patient does not exist soon emerges. Instead, there are often several sensible directions to pursue, each of which has advantages and disadvantages. The student may choose one suitable to the relationship between the patient and himself and acceptable to both. Part of the work is to acquire the capacity to think, to make hypotheses, test them and see the results. This is often seen by teachers as a vague area and is defended against, usually by the doctor taking up rigid attitudes to his work.

It can be very hard for the student to begin to find his place in the clinical scenario. Doctors, nurses and patients all have a seemingly well-defined role on the hospital stage. The student often feels that he is only a burden to the patients and staff, someone who is in the way. It is common for students to be concerned at over-exposing an ill person to yet another clerk or examination. Certainly this may be true when a patient is treated as a body with a particular pathology, the self that is someone with feelings and sensitivities to the medical process, being ignored. Yet this common undervaluing by the student of himself is erroneous. The patient often relishes the attendance of the student as the only one whom he can actually talk with. All the trained staff may appear to be, or actually are, too busy to spend time in thinking with the patient about what is happening. This is precisely the position of the student who is also trying to assimilate what is going on. This common interest may enable the patient to divulge a much richer tapestry of findings than the plain somatic component. Each patient has a story to tell, has feelings about what is happening and, especially, phantasies of what is inside his body and what will be its outcome.

The sensitive student may quickly find that he has become a repository of knowledge about the anxieties of the patient and how his problems began. He may have been told for instance of the elderly patient's concern for his dog, his only companion for many years. Dealing with such a 'tiny' human problem may lead to a great lessening of the patient's anxiety, increase the therapeutic alliance and substantially alter the patient's feelings about his doctor and his medical treatment. *Yet it needs to be listened to.* And the student must be able to speak up for the psychological aspects of the patient's hospitalization.

He may find that the man with a myocardial infarction had his chest pain immediately following a row with his wife. Further investigation of the social system will reveal a marriage full of fights, with the husband's comment to his wife, clutching his chest in pain, 'You'll be the death of me.' Thus, there is a social and human context of the pathology of the heart. It may be necessary for marital therapy to be prescribed, as much as physical treatment for the damaged heart, this specific symptom being a metaphor for the pain of love.

Another example would be the patient who is only able to talk of impending death with the student and not with other staff who may 'know' and who perhaps are unable to face the pain of such a discussion. The student may find himself specifically caught by the patient in order to have an audience for his fears and preoccupations. The former may only have an imperfect knowledge of the medical position and yet he can contribute a great deal to the psychological needs of the patient at such times. This is a crucial period for the student who must take a personal decision about the psyche-soma. Will he identify with the consultants and trained staff in seeing medicine as an emotionally detached issue, ignoring the psychic pain of the patient and passing by? The alternative is to begin to know that the patient is a human being with a history of life and feelings and anxieties about his present predicament which need to be taken into account. The argument usually runs that this 'soft-end' of medicine takes up too much time. Such a rationalization is untrue. The point is that the patient can be regarded as invisible, the body being only the container of pathology and illness, or experienced as a human being. Often the student can learn to be really in touch with the patient, a process often shunned because the qualified doctor may not be able to face the depression, the consequences perhaps of failure of medicine and the pain of sharing knowledge about feelings of what is happening. Yet the very act of being touched by a patient psychologically and, in return, letting the patient know that his anxieties and affects are understood, constitutes the essence of the Art of Healing.

● **Reference**

Balint M., Balint E., Gosling R. et al. (1966) *The Study of Doctors*. Mind and Medicine Monographs Series.

4

Psychotherapy in liaison psychiatry

by Chris Thomas

• Introduction

Liaison psychiatry is a new term for a relatively old concept. It can be described as the activities carried out by a psychiatrist when working in the non-psychiatric departments of a general hospital. Usually, this involves the psychiatrist with patients who are suffering, or appear to be suffering, from physical illnesses. The term 'liaison' implies that a major aspect of this work is for the psychiatrist to share his findings, opinions and therapeutic suggestions with the medical and nursing staff who are primarily involved in managing the patient.

It is becoming increasingly apparent that the purely biological approach to medicine is not sufficient and, to understand fully any patient, a wider perspective must be adopted that involves consideration of emotional and environmental factors, as well as physical aspects. New terms such as 'holistic medicine' or the 'biopsychosocial model' are being used to describe an approach to patient care whose origin goes back to Ancient Greece. These views perhaps tended to be overlooked in the last 100 years when, in a new scientific age, the biological aspects of disease undoubtedly took many steps forward. Now, however, awareness is returning that not all aspects of illness can be explained biologically and that both the causes and results of illness are multifactorial.

It could be argued that, if patients should be viewed with this multifactorial approach, then it would be wrong to have a psychiatrist involved with the psychological and emotional factors and that any doctor should be able to deal with all aspects. In the majority of cases this should apply and only in occasional situations would a psychiatrist be needed, when psychological considerations are particularly great and the doctor managing the patient may feel that he himself does not have sufficient knowledge or skills.

A liaison psychiatrist may become involved in many different problems that occur in general hospital patients, including organic cerebral states, self-poisoning, eating disorders, hysterical conversion states and abnormal illness behaviours. All of these problems may also present to a general psychiatrist and do not require different knowledge or skills from those already outlined in this book. There is one aspect of liaison psychiatry, however, that constitutes a major source of referrals, does not often present to a general psychiatrist and may require different skills. This is the area of psychological reactions to physical illness and the rest of this chapter will concentrate on this.

• Therapeutic Needs of Liaison Psychiatry

If a liaison psychiatrist is to deal effectively with the wide range of problems that is referred to him, then he will need a variety of different therapeutic interventions. If he is firmly entrenched in either a pharmacological, behavioural or psychotherapeutic model of treatment, then there is likely to be a number of patients who will not benefit from referral. With each patient, the liaison psychiatrist must decide whether treatment will be most effective by using drugs, behavioural techniques, psychotherapy or, perhaps most commonly, a combination of these therapies.

Psychotherapeutic skills will undoubtedly be needed by the liaison psychiatrist and it would not be unreasonable to suggest that psychotherapy will be needed in varying degrees at some stage in the management of all his referrals. In liaison psychiatry, psychotherapy can be used at three different levels — the psychotherapeutically-orientated interview, supportive psychotherapy and insight-orientated psychotherapy. These different levels use different techniques and are employed to achieve different goals. There is no reason with general medical patients why a psychotherapeutically-orientated interview cannot be used by any doctor without any specialized training, and supportive psychotherapy can be undertaken by most doctors after acquiring some basic skills. Insight-orientated psychotherapy, on the other hand, can usually only be used in general medicine by staff such as psychiatrists who have had specialized training and will not often be utilized by the medical staff themselves.

The basic goal of a normal clinical interview with a medical patient is to enable the doctor to obtain enough information to help him arrive at a diagnosis and plan the management. It is, therefore, a process largely for the benefit of the doctor. *The psychotherapeutically-orientated interview* is designed as a modification of the usual clinical history-taking, whereby not only the doctor, but also the patient benefits from the interaction. It has the goal of not only obtaining information, but also of feeding information back and establishing a rapport and a therapeutic alliance. At the end of the interview, the doctor will not only know about the illness, but will also know the patient and the way he feels about his problems; the patient will feel not only diagnosed, but also understood. Many doctors will claim that this is not psychotherapy but just good clinical practice which they exercize all the time. It *is* psychotherapy, albeit in a simple form, because during the interview the doctor will explore feelings, beliefs and attitudes and may outline to the patient certain features in his personality and background that explain why symptoms or illnesses have developed. The patient hopefully will be able to use this information in a constructive way to help him understand more about himself and perhaps even make some changes in his feelings or behaviour that lead to some relief of physical symptoms. Even in a single interview, a patient may feel accepted and valued by a doctor who shows an empathic awareness of his problems. If this occurs, the patient is more likely to feel safe about discussing fears and anxieties and, if these can be verbalized at the time, he may begin to evaluate them and obtain a sense of relief. The psychotherapeutically-orientated interview can occur on every occasion that a doctor sees the patient and it does not require a set number of sessions. Indeed, it can often be used successfully with just one meeting.

In liaison psychiatry, *supportive psychotherapy* is often considered useful. Physical illness often represents a crisis and, not surprisingly, emotional health may be affected. In acute illnesses, patients may require emotional support from other people, either until recovery or until death. If the illness is chronic, or its consequences permanent, then support may be needed over a much longer period until acceptance of the illness has occurred. The skills needed are a development of those used in the psychotherapeutically-orientated interview and, providing they are willing to give the time, there is no reason why the vast majority of doctors should not be able to offer supportive psychotherapy to their patients. During this form of psychotherapy the doctor is not concerned with factual information about the illness but concentrates on *listening* to the patient talking about the problems and, especially, about the fears and consequences of the illness. Helping the patient verbalize these is the doctor's main task. This process continues over a number of sessions rather than just a single interview, so that the patient can continue to build up a trust in the doctor, allowing them both to explore issues that may have remained hidden in early interviews. As well as verbalization of anxieties, the doctor should help the patient explore ways in which the problems and feelings can be dealt with more effectively. In many situations, it may not only be the patient that requires supportive psychotherapy: physical illness affects the whole family and all members may suffer and require support from medical staff. Also, in certain medical units, the pressures on staff may be enormous, due to the exacting and emotionally harrowing nature of their work. Consideration may, therefore, need to be given to the provision of support to the *staff* on these units.

Dynamic psychotherapy is intended to help people come to understand, and eventually change, certain aspects of themselves by the gradual uncovering of unconscious motivations and defences and potentially it is of great use, at least in some of its aspects, in managing patients with physical illness. In some people, the reactions to physical illness may seem exaggerated or even quite different from those normally shown by patients with the disease. These atypical reactions may be a result of unconscious factors in the patient, rather than a pure response to the stress of the disease process and then psychotherapy may require dynamic as well as supportive approaches to help the patient change to a more normal emotional response. Dynamic psychotherapy may be time-consuming, requiring many sessions and its use will thus be restricted; part of a liaison psychiatrist's job will be to assess which patients may benefit most from dynamic therapy and to concentrate on offering it effectively to such patients.

• Psychological Reactions to Physical Illness

All patients have feelings and thoughts about their disease and treatment and, therefore, all illnesses will be associated with various psychological reactions. Many reactions will be minor, but in a few instances there may be a severe reaction that causes problems in its own right, separate from the physical distress of the illness itself. Sometimes, the reaction produces a problem that affects relatives or hospital staff more than the patient himself. The severity of the psychological reaction is usually dependent on how threatening the illness is perceived to be. This, in turn, will depend on factors in three areas — the disease itself, the person concerned and the situation produced. Certain illnesses are commonly perceived as being threatening to the sufferer, particularly those where the patient believes there is a risk of death, severe disability, prolonged pain, a mutilating outcome or unpleasant treatment. Not surprisingly, many people with illnesses carrying these risks frequently have profound psychological reactions (although they are often well controlled and even hidden from medical staff). As well as factors in the disease itself, the threat of an illness will be influenced by aspects of the person suffering it. The various reactions that a given patient has developed in the past for dealing with stress will play an important role in shaping his or her psychological reaction to illness. A person who believes he has control over situations may develop a more positive, 'fighting' approach to serious illness that will help lower distress, whereas someone who feels they have no power to deal with stressful situations and are in the hands of fate may suffer severe emotional disturbance with the same illness. The previous awareness the patient has of the disease will also affect response. A woman with an abnormal cervical smear who has a relative still alive ten years after a cone biopsy will view her disease quite differently from one who recalls a relative dying with disseminated carcinomatosis within a few months of the same procedure. In psychotherapy, with the physically ill, it is therefore essential that the doctor explores the background, attitudes and beliefs of the patients as well as knowledge about how they have coped with illnesses and other stresses in the past. The other factors that determine the threat of the illness, apart from those of the disease and the sufferer, will depend on the situation that may result from it. Certain illnesses may not in themselves be threatening, but may nevertheless interfere considerably with the patient's ability to perform normal roles and relationships. The financial, occupational, leisure, marital, sexual and parental consequences may be more distressing than the physical effects of the illness. A man may tolerate an epileptic fit itself, but if his job had depended on a car, then the loss of his licence will cause major problems.

Psychotherapy with the physically ill will require the exploration of all the factors that may play a part in shaping the psychological response. It is of great importance that the therapist does not start with preconceived ideas about the stresses that the patient suffers. Some women with carcinoma of the breast may cope with the stress of the cancer, its possible recurrence and even perhaps their own death, but be devastated by the 'mutilation' of losing a breast, whereas other women feel the surgeons can 'cut out' whatever they like and will tolerate severely mutilating procedures because the stress of having cancer inside them is quite intolerable. The therapist needs to outline with the patient the exact stresses and also to be prepared that these may change. As the disease progresses, different stresses may arise that need psychotherapeutic attention in different ways.

The form of the psychological response to a threatening illness will, in many patients, be a mood disturbance such as anxiety and depression. However, in some, the psychological reaction will be exhibited as a defence mechanism that the patient utilizes to reduce the potential mood disturbance.

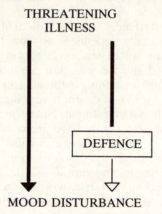

The psychotherapist will soon need to gauge the severity of any mood disturbance and to decide which, if any, of the defences the patient is using. He will also have to decide whether the defence is effective and should be encouraged, or whether it is causing problems that are worse than the mood disturbance it tries to prevent and, therefore, should be tackled through psychotherapy.

● **Anxiety and Depression**

The majority of patients with a threatening illness will at some stage show evidence of anxiety or depression and this is usually quite understandable and does not require specific psychiatric intervention. Anxiety results from uncertainty, whereas depression is the result of unpleasant knowledge. Many illnesses carry both uncertainty and unpleasant facts and most patients show features of both mood disturbances. Nevertheless, it is unreasonable to assume that because it is 'normal' it does not require attention. The attention it requires is in the form of supportive psychotherapy that can be carried out by any doctor, nurse or even student and may not require much time.

The first part of the psychotherapeutic management is to recognise the distress. This involves not only direct questions about mood, but also observing and commenting on non-verbal responses of the patient that indicate underlying disturbances. In some patients it may be appropriate actually to suggest that they *should* feel upset, if it appears as though they are hiding their feelings, and such a comment might release a considerable amount of pent-up emotion. The therapist should then allow the patient time to talk about all his fears and depressive feelings without too many interruptions. The simple procedure of allowing patients the chance and time to 'get problems off their chest' is a very powerful aid in supportive psychotherapy. Following this, the therapist should try to explain the reactions the patient is having in terms of what he knows about the illness and the person; again, it can be very reassuring for a patient to have his mood disturbance understood by another person. The patient should be helped to realise that he is not alone in his feelings, that others have felt the same and he is not unusual or mad. Usually associated with this understanding is an implied *permission* that he is allowed to feel the way he does. Occasionally, patients think they are not allowed to be upset and believe medical staff would be angry if they openly showed emotions. (Unfortunately, they are sometimes correct in this belief.) In psychotherapy, 'permission' is given for the patient to be open about his feelings to himself as well as to the therapist. The patient should also be given permission to continue to feel distressed and know that the therapist realises the stresses will be present for some time and that talking about them does not make them disappear. Thus the therapist conveys to the patient his *acceptance* of his feelings in an uncritical manner. In further sessions, the therapist may feel disappointed that the patient appears to go over the same ground continually, but in supportive psychotherapy this is often important. By repeated talking about stresses and release of associated emotions, the patient gradually adapts and the depression and anxiety diminish. To aid this process, it is occasionally useful to encourage the patient to share his feelings with other people, especially his family. In lengthy illnesses, the therapist will also help the patient look at stresses that may arise in the future, so they can be worked on and sorted out before they give rise to emotional disturbance.

A few patients will have mood disturbances that are less understandable in that they are very severe or last longer than usual and may require more specialized attention. Sometimes, they can be helped with supportive psychotherapy and the addition of psychotropic drugs or behavioural techniques, but others may require more intensive dynamic psychotherapy. This more intensive psychotherapy helps the patient explore underlying reasons for an excessive reaction. Patients sometimes believe they are responsible for their illnesses and occasionally view the illness as a justified punishment for past failings. This leads them to believe the illness is deserved and their prolonged depression becomes a form of penance. Other patients may, through their own illness, re-experience the feelings and emotions that were associated with the ill health and death of other people, such as parents, and their prolonged depression can be understood as a form of delayed grief. Sometimes, a severe or lengthy mood disturbance is the result of feelings that their life has been wasted and they have unfulfilled ambitions and dreams that will never now come to fruition. All these sorts of problems may require delicate handling in a more protracted psychotherapeutic relationship.

●   **Denial**
Denial is often the first reaction a patient shows when he first has to face a threatening illness. Providing it does not last too long, it is a normal and understandable defence that prevents the patient from being flooded with severe emotions at a stage when he is not yet ready to deal with them. Denial can be used

both against facts and also against the emotions associated with the facts. Initially, the patient may deny the diagnosis or its seriousness. He may believe the doctors are wrong and this occasionally leads the patient to not believing the medical staff and to request a second opinion. This denial of facts does not usually last for more than two to three weeks but is occasionally accompanied by a longer denial of feelings wherein the patient accepts his diagnosis, but reports a state of numbness or emotional emptiness. During this phase, he has great difficulty in experiencing the appropriate degree of depression or anxiety that the illness would be expected to produce. Over time, the numbness gradually reduces, to be replaced by understandable depression and anxiety. Denial in this sense is therefore a useful and necessary defence allowing the patient a period of time to accept gradually the situation he is faced with and to find other defences to cope with the psychological distress. This early and relatively short-lived denial should therefore not be removed psychotherapeutically and it would be cruel to make the patient face facts and emotions before he is ready. The medical staff should gently present the facts as they know them to the patients and allow them to question them. It is important that, if the patient appears to disbelieve or want another opinion, the doctor should not feel this is a personal attack and therefore become angry, but should understand the patient's need to assimilate slowly the information as the denial decreases.

In some patients, denial may last much longer and become a very poor defence. In these cases, the patient may refuse to believe that his illness is serious or even that it is present at all, and this may prevent him complying with therapy and occasionally even stop him seeing doctors at all, which obviously puts him at risk. It is important in these instances to try and gently penetrate the denial, using psychotherapy, so that the patient accepts correct treatment. Even if the patient allows the medical team to carry out treatment, denial over a long period may cause hardship to a family, as the patient will be prevented from perhaps making necessary arrangements, in case his illness becomes terminal. It may also prevent the family talking with him, over important issues that they feel need to be discussed. In these cases, if the family wish it, psychotherapy may be needed to help the patient drop the denial. If the denial, however, is not interfering with treatment or upsetting the family, then the therapist must seriously consider whether it is best left untouched if it is successfully preventing anxiety and depression and allowing the patient to cope.

It is also important to realise that some terminal or chronic patients have fully come to terms with their illnesses and disabilities and have decided not to talk about them and to live the rest of their lives without continually being concerned about their health. This may at first appear to be denial but obviously is not and it would be inappropriate to try to alter this form of coping through psychotherapy.

● Anger

Another common reaction to serious illness is anger, which may first appear when denial fades. During this phase, the patient tries to find someone or something to blame for his predicament. Often, the blame will be levelled at the medical or nursing staff, who may be accused quite unfairly of missing the diagnosis, delaying treatment or purposefully providing false information. At the same time, close relatives and friends may be criticized and told that the illness is their fault because of past stresses they have subjected the patient to. Some people turn their anger towards God for allowing the illness to fall upon them. Even strangers can be blamed for being well, whilst the patient suffers and a frequent complaint at this time is, 'Why me?'. This anger is again an understandable defence when the patient is slowly becoming aware of the full facts of his diagnosis and prognosis. It gives the patient a sense of unfairness but provides him with an aggressive, fighting attitude rather than allowing him to sink into a state of hopelessness and inactive depression. In the majority of people, it does not last too long and one of the main tasks of a therapist will be to help other staff and relatives understand the process and to reassure them that it will pass and the patients will not carry grievances for the rest of their lives. It is important that those involved with the patient listen to his anger and empathize with him, without actually agreeing that people have been at fault. Whilst listening, alternative explanations can be offered if the patient has misconceptions about the causes or management of his illness, but outright arguing with the patient should be avoided as this will lead to confrontation which may seem to confirm his belief that others have wronged him. It may be possible to get the patient to shift the aggressive attitude away from other people onto the actual disease process itself and this may help him develop a positive approach with a belief of being able to fight and thus overcome the illness. Patients who develop this fighting spirit towards the illness usually manage to cope well from a psychological view point.

Unfortunately, in a small number of seriously ill people, anger becomes a fixed defence leading to a permanent sense of unfairness and aggression towards others. This tends to lead to major breakdowns in the relationships between the patient and his medical carers, his relatives and his friends and they may become permanently isolated. It is tragic when a person dies alone because all his contacts have been driven from him by his chronic anger and, if this seems to be occurring, it is a very deserving situation for a psychotherapeutic approach. The therapist must show the patient that he can accept his anger and then try to persuade him to look at the feelings it is preventing. This ultimately involves the therapist in exploring the underlying depression and anxiety and perhaps helps the patient to cry and be despairing. Hopefully, with psychotherapy, the severity of the depression can be worked through so that the patient gradually accepts both the illness and the people who wish to be close to him whilst he is ill. Sometimes psychotherapy reveals that the purpose of anger is actually to drive someone very close away from the patient, so as to prevent them from being hurt. The patient may believe that if he antagonizes a relative prior to his death, the relative will not suffer in the bereavement. The patient needs help to realise that this is rarely successful because usually the relative will grieve even more if they have not been close together in the final stages of the illness. In these situations the therapist may need to work with both patient and relative.

• Independence and Dependence

In many patients there is a desire to remain independent as far as possible and only to use the services of the hospital when it is essential; this reaction is usually encouraged. Occasionally, a patient's independence may become out of proportion and, as with denial, may lead to rejecting perhaps vital treatment. A patient may, for example, refuse analgesics even though he is in pain. Sometimes, independence in hospital leads to subjects failing to co-operate with the routine most patients accept as a necessary part of the smooth running of the ward. Heart patients may continue to smoke, or diabetic patients repeatedly to ignore their dietary restrictions. Independence can lead patients to reject offers of aid from family or friends and they struggle on, coping less and less well but refusing to allow anyone to help. This behaviour is very distressing for the families who see the people developing more and more problems but not letting them become involved.

Psychotherapy will often be needed where independence is quite out of proportion to the situation. In some patients the problem can be resolved by helping to show them that allowing others to help is not a sign of weakness or 'giving in' to the illness. Occasionally, the problem is due to longstanding beliefs, and intensive insight-orientated psychotherapy may reveal that they are people who have never allowed anyone to control them and have always fought against authority. These patients need help to see that treatment is not a conflict situation between them and the doctors, but a joint effort on both sides to combat the illness.

Dependence is the opposite reaction to independence and occurs when patients allow the hospital or family to take over all aspects of their illness and take no personal control of it themselves. They will show no effort really to fight the disease and may show poor co-operation with all attempts at rehabilitation. It may get so severe that the patient remains bed-bound, becomes incontinent and requires feeding by others, without adequate physical reasons. This form of reaction in patients may be an attempt to protect themselves from underlying emotions by allowing other people to be responsible for the illness and therefore letting them do the worrying. As with independence, some patients show a habitual pattern of responding this way. In the past, whenever problems occurred, they regressed to the position of being a child and this allowed others to act in a parental way. Such people may never have become fully independent of their parents and may require detailed psychotherapy.

In physical illness, therefore, successful coping allows a patient to be independent in many areas of his life, but can also allow him to depend on others when the need arises.

● **Acting Out**

Many patients deal with the anxiety of their illness by obtaining attention and sympathy from others. A few people find it too anxiety-provoking for others to concentrate on their illness and may try to obtain the equivalent degree of attention by utilizing highly abnormal behaviour patterns. This is known as acting out. It may involve excessive use of drink or drugs, lying, destructive acts, criminality or promiscuous behaviour. As the hospital staff or family will find these behaviours quite unacceptable, they will attempt to control them and it is while they impose the control that the patient will obtain the attention, even though it may be in the form of 'punishment'. These forms of behaviour will, therefore, change the whole focus of attention of both the patient and his attendants away from the physical disease onto the abnormal activity and reduce the anxiety of being ill.

Psychotherapy is usually urgently needed in these cases to prevent severe deterioration of relationships between the patient and his medical team. The staff should have the patient's behaviour explained to them and be advised that if attention is not given to the maladaptive behaviour it will tend to diminish. With the patient, the therapist will try to establish a relationship which provides the attention he is seeking, and then to explore gradually the real anxieties and concerns that the illness imposes. This may in some cases be exceedingly difficult, as the patient ultimately destroys all attempts by the therapist to engage in a proper relationship.

- **Over-confiding and Over-involvement**

A common way of dealing with any stress is to gather knowledge about the problem and to discuss it with others to see whether solutions can be found. All patients use this method to at least some extent. In a few, this may be taken to extreme levels and become harmful. The patient may read many books about his disease and often concentrates on the worst interpretation. By questioning many members of staff he will normally obtain slightly different information from each one and then he becomes concerned about what he considers to be major discrepancies and assumes that something is being hidden from him. This process, rather than lowering anxiety and depression, may actually increase it.

Similarly, the patients may seek many people in whom to confide and continuously seek reassurance from them. Again, discrepancies may heighten psychological distress. Whereas relatives or friends are usually happy to listen to problems for a certain period of time, they expect that eventually the patient will adjust and talk less of his illness and more about other matters. If the patient over-confides, he may actually drive the person away and start to experience antagonism and rejection, which leads to more, rather than less, psychological disturbance.

In these cases, psychotherapy needs to be quite directive in preventing patients seeking information from many places and one person (preferably a senior member of the medical team) should be identified as the only source. The psychotherapist will usually allow himself to be the one person who will counsel the patient and help him work through his anxieties so that he does not need continual reassurance from other people

- **Displacement**

Another method by which anxiety may be dealt with is to remove it from its real source and transfer it to some other concern. A patient using this defence, called displacement, may deny any anxieties about his real illness but become preoccupied with another body part, a non-illness-related situation, or even another person. A person with cancer may claim he has fully come to terms with it but may continuously complain of pain in another site for which no organic pathology is found. Alternatively, he may become extremely preoccupied with a minor stress at work or in a relationship that previously would not have worried him. Perhaps the commonest form of displacement is when the patient starts to worry about other people, often complaining that it is the relatives who need help to come to term with the illness, not himself. In hospital, patients may displace their anxieties by making unwarranted accusations that the staff have mishandled or ignored another patient. They may try to help all the other patients and even try to usurp the nursing and medical staff by taking on their functions. These patients then become very hurt when the staff try to curb their excessive over-concern with the other patients.

Some patients may join self-help groups and use their displacement to become counsellors themselves. Patients who have genuinely come to terms with their illness may be extremely useful in counselling others with the same problem, but if the feelings have not been worked through and helping others is due to displacement of the counsellors' own anxiety then they usually become over-involved with the person they are trying to help, lose objectivity and cause more harm than good.

Psychotherapy is difficult to carry out with these patients because they refuse to admit any anxieties about their own illness and insist the problems lie elsewhere. If they *can* be engaged in a relationship, the therapist has to try gradually to persuade the patients to examine the real underlying concern about their illness and more appropriately replace the displaced anxiety, and then to work with them in dealing with it more appropriately.

● **Conclusion**

The majority of people who have to experience a serious illness during their lives are likely at some stage to show one or more of the reactions described in this chapter. All patients, therefore, require psychotherapeutic support and understanding, though in the vast majority of cases this can be adequately provided by their own families and their normal medical attendants. Only occasionally will a liaison psychiatrist be required to carry out more intensive psychotherapeutic treatment.

Hopefully, the majority of patients will eventually come to some degree of acceptance of their illness and many will adopt coping strategies and defences that are entirely successful and will never require any intervention and for this reason they have not been mentioned in the chapter. If all patients with physical disease are considered from the physical, psychological and social viewpoint at the same time, then it is probable that there will be a much higher degree of satisfaction in the treatment and care that they receive whilst in the hands of doctors and other medical staff.

5

Psychotherapy in general practice
'Hearing secret harmonies' (Anthony Powell)

by Andrew Elder

● **The Setting**

Specialized psychotherapy is concerned with the treatment of selected patients in a highly organized setting. The treatment of patients in general practice is very different. The surgery doors open onto the everyday world. In general practice the doctor is not set at such a careful distance, monitoring the various aspects of transference and projection, but enmeshed, a fellow traveller, more involved with his patients and their illnesses. It is High Street medicine. This difference gives rise to many of the difficulties of the setting, but also to some of its unique advantages for psychotherapeutic work. In general practice the doctor is not concerned with the application of any particular therapeutic philosophy, but more with whatever psychotherapeutic use he can make of the opportunities that arise as part of his everyday work. He is an *opportunist*. He carries with him whatever skills and awareness he possesses in whatever he is called on to do — visiting a dying patient at home, dealing with a 'minor' illness in the surgery, responding to an emotional crisis, or a problem concealed in a 'While I'm here, Doctor'. The general practitioner's psychotherapy is dressed in ordinary clothing.

Psychoanalytic theory gives us an essentially developmental view of human life, placing 'each individual in his own unique cultural and developmental context' (Brown and Pedder 1979) and lays great emphasis on the quality of the human relationships that enable the individual's development from the earliest moments of life. Difficulties and conflicts, as well as satisfactions and achievements, are constantly present and may build up in such a way that a crisis or an illness develops. For a few patients this may lead to formal psychotherapy, but for the overwhelming majority it is neither sought nor appropriate. The doctor in general practice, however, is often already present at first hand, helping his patients with many of these experiences that are some of the psychological determinants of people's lives: the problems of birth and early childhood, sexual development and marriage, illnesses, death and losses of one sort or another. Morbidity and presentations to the doctor are known to increase when people are negotiating these major transitions of life, or life events. This means that the

47

doctor is often involved when psychic history is being made. He can therefore influence this process, a little, both for better and for worse.

- ● **Listening**

    In this chapter I shall often refer to listening and hearing when describing the need for doctors to 'listen' to their patients and 'hear' what they are saying. This does not mean a passive process of sitting back and listening to someone talk. It refers to the quality and intensity of the listening to feelings that lie behind the patient's words, and the sensitivity with which things are heard that the patient is only half saying. This requires considerable attention to detail; how the patient looks and behaves, his mood, what words he chooses, when he falters and changes tack and what is left unsaid; it involves respecting the patient's need to express emotion in his own way and hearing what thoughts and feelings all these things, and many more, elicit in the doctor's own mind.

    Most communication from which something new may be learnt by the person communicating exists in a half-lit world of things that are only 'almost known' to that person. This is true of the patient communicating to his doctor and also true of the doctor when he attempts any change in his understanding of his patients or his involvement with them. Both worlds, the patient's and the doctor's, are changing. It is the relationship between the two, referred to in this chapter as the doctor-patient relationship, that is of central importance.

- ● **Incidence**

    It is a commonplace that the incidence of emotional or psychiatric disorders seen in general practice is high. Figures vary widely; the problems of definition are great and the diagnoses made in general practice consultations depend as much on the doctor's own characteristics and attitudes, as on the patient's presentation. In a practice with a special interest in psychological disorders, 43 per cent of all patients seen had symptoms which were regarded as being of emotional origin; 11 per cent suffered from formal psychiatric illnesses and 32 per cent from a variety of stress disorders (Hopkins 1956). In another survey (Goldberg and Blackwell 1970), a general practitioner, who was again described as having a particular interest in psychiatric disorders, only recorded an incidence of 20 per cent of consecutive attenders as having evidence of psychiatric morbidity. It may be that another doctor, steadfastly physical in his approach and determined not to notice his patients' emotional problems, could achieve a significantly lower incidence still. Doctors are as variable as their patients.

    Despite these differences in the doctors' diagnostic thresholds, it seems that the average general practitioner in this country is likely to have a significant number of his consultations, probably averaging around 30 per cent (*Royal College of General Practioners* 1981) with people who have been propelled towards the surgery by apparent psychiatric symptomatology of one sort or another. This figure may rise to 60 per cent or more if consultations are included in which the doctor feels there is a significant element of emotional difficulty being presented.

Some people consult their general practitioners much more often than others. Approximately 50 per cent of the general practitioner's workload is generated by 10 per cent of his patients (Jarman et al. 1985). The members of each doctor's 10 per cent group may have more psychological characteristics in common with each other than with less frequently consulting patients who may, nevertheless, belong to the same diagnostic category (for instance, migraine, dysmenorrhoea or depression). Amongst the population who do not go to the doctor often are individuals who have similar symptoms as those who do (Miller et al. 1976). It is not the possession of the symptom or the disorder that characterizes the patients who more frequently come to the surgery, but the fact that they come, while others do not. This realization is vital to the general practitioner's work.

• **What Kind of Diagnosis?**

Although the results of these surveys give us something of a statistical background to the general practitioner's work, they do so in misleading terms. Diagnoses of this sort belong to a psychiatric classification derived from what is often called the medical model. The doctor presides, uninvolved with his patient, and diagnoses the patient's illness according to certain symptoms and signs. Such a model encourages the doctor to think only about making the 'right' diagnosis and not about the patient, and inclines both the patient and the doctor to define the problem outside themselves, thus discouraging the doctor from thinking about his relationship with the patient. It is a model much used in hospital thinking, but it transfers very uneasily into general practice, where the emphasis is shifted more to people and away from illnesses; more to a longer term perspective rather than a two-dimensional view at one moment. It makes little sense to place two totally different consultations with people of different personalities and backgrounds with different problems and expectations into a single category called, say, anxiety state.

> A large woman in her sixties, who always has a timid look about her, comes to see the doctor about her painful neck which prevents her from sleeping. She is a bit overweight, tends to visit the doctor about once a month and is recently retired from her work as a cleaner. She comes to ask for a repeat of her arthritis tablets and wonders if her blood pressure is up (which it is, slightly). She cries when the doctor asks about her brother whom he knows she has been worried about and who is now dying of cancer. She is single, rather shy and has always felt large and awkward. She has remained closely attached to her large number of brothers and sisters since their father died when she was nine. They mostly live a long way from her and she is constantly anxious about them. The doctor has got to know her and how she uses him. He is happy to see her and takes her blood pressure, listens to her and prescribes more tablets. The consultation lasts ten minutes and will be repeated many times, in one form or another, as it already has been in the past.

Such a consultation is very typical of a general practitioner's work. Which diagnosis is the doctor to choose? Even sticking to traditional medical diagnoses, it would be difficult to choose between obesity, mild hypertension, cervical spondylosis, anxiety or depression. All play a part.

If we shift the emphasis from the medical diagnosis towards a more personal one, we immediately begin to include some life history, any important recent events, present tensions with other people and something of the patient's relationship to herself; her self-esteem and confidence, and her capacity for change and adaptation. These things may help us learn more about her emotional needs and what she may require from a visit to the doctor. The single page becomes biography.

It does, however, still leave out any account of the doctor's own particular viewpoint. The importance of this omission increases as the patient's subjective world is taken more into account. The diagnosis has to broaden again to include something of the doctor's own reactions and how he sees the patient. Today's view may be different tomorrow and the same patient would be seen differently by different doctors.

- #### Knocking on the Doctor's Door

Amongst the sea of people who come in and out of a doctor's surgery, some people will have a relatively clear idea of why they have come and what they can reasonably hope to gain. Others are propelled by a less well-differentiated urge, a more generalized need for understanding or help, which they initially transmit to the doctor through their symptoms. These may resolve quite quickly or continue until the doctor and patient eventually settle on a distance and a language that is acceptable to both of them. This is then the 'illness'. It is particularly important for the doctor in general practice to tolerate uncertainty and not organize the patient's illness too soon. He may otherwise prevent important developments from emerging and contribute to what Illich has called the 'medicalization of life'. The groundswell of need which brings people to doctors is present in everyone. For some, it is more successfully met in life relationships than for others. The doctor is a relatively freely available figure. Maybe in previous times, such a need sought its expression elsewhere, through the church or within the extended family, but in today's world it knocks on the doctor's door. Both the patient and the doctor contain numerous possibilities for the outcome of their consultation together. They each have the potential for many different directions and levels of contact with each other. Nothing is static. Patients alter their patterns to fit their doctors and seek out doctors who reflect their needs. For many patients it may be more important that there is a channel of communication open to them when they need it, rather than its particular medical content.

Doctors develop different ways of responding to this challenge. Each doctor's own approach may be valid for himself. There is a risk in too great a conformity. If a doctor does decide to undergo appropriate training and learn to make himself more accessible to his patient's emotional needs, he must first become aware of the history and development of the thought that has already gone into trying to understand the nature of the general practice setting for this kind of work.

- **History**

The history of psychotherapy in general practice is essentially the history of the impact of two psychoanalysts, Michael and Enid Balint, and their work with general practitioners. The story begins with general practice at a low ebb in the early 1950s, very much the junior partner within the medical profession. There was 'widespread dissatisfaction amongst general practitioners' (Collings 1950) who at that time lacked any specific training for their work. The mismatch between the skills acquired through undergraduate medical training and those needed by the general practitioner in his work was even more acute then than it is now. Apart from their heavily disease-centred training, those doctors had mainly their common sense and endless outpatient referrals to help them through.

In 1948 at the Tavistock Clinic in London, Enid Balint began leading a group of non-medical workers who were working with people having marital difficulties. Michael Balint, a Hungarian psychoanalyst whose father had been a family doctor, became interested in applying this method to study the difficulties general practitioners were having and to see if new techniques could be developed to help them in their work. In 1954 and 1955 the first reports of this work were published (Balint 1954 and 1955). It initiated far-reaching changes in the ways doctors and patients were subsequently to relate to each other. Much was learnt from this early work and was eventually published in 1957 as *The Doctor, His Patient and the Illness* (Balint 1957), one of the masterpieces of medical literature.

From the beginning, this work was a marriage between the psychoanalytical background of the Balints and the medical work and attitudes brought to the groups by those first general practitioners.

The Balints contributed the setting, the aims, the open-mindedness of their enquiry and a belief in the value of human beings (doctors as well as patients). They also contributed their understanding of the unconscious and a basic trust that, from the ruminations of the doctors themselves, new patterns would emerge. They were non-moralizing and non-didactic. They did not attempt to instruct the doctors in psychoanalytic theory or give them psychodynamic explanations of their patients' behaviour, or of the doctors' own behaviour for that matter. Through their own listening skills, enhanced by psychoanalytic training, they helped the doctors listen better to their patients. Winnicott and others have shown how a mother can respond more sensitively to her child if she has herself received what he called 'good-enough mothering' (Winnicott 1972). By the same token, doctors are better able to respond to their patients' problems if they have had the experience of being listened to sensitively themselves in their training. They are then able to learn more from the main source and stimulus to education for doctors, that is, *the patients themselves*.

The doctors also had much to contribute. They brought their openness and willingness to learn, which is never an easy process, and their preparedness to stick at a difficult task for a considerable length of time. They required what Balint came to call the 'courage of their stupidity' (Balint 1957). This meant being prepared to use their minds imaginatively and contribute freely to the thinking of the group; not being too cautious and correct. This courage remains the main driving force for any group.

• Training

The method of work and its aims have remained essentially the same over the years. A small group of general practitioners meet each week with a suitably trained leader and present cases that are giving them difficulty. They do so without notes which enables the doctor to give a more spontaneous presentation, disclosing to the group some of his own subjective reactions to the patient. With the help of the leader(s), the group then examines the doctor's and the patient's interactions over the whole of their relationship, and also focussing on the detail of a recent consultation:

'Why did you do that?'; 'How did she react?'; 'I feel that by prescribing for her at that moment, you were dismissing her'; 'I don't think this patient can get through to you'; 'I think you were caught in a difficult situation'; etc.

> 'The doctor comes to the group with the real burden of a difficult case. In reporting his case and joining in the discussion, he tests his own ideas against those of his colleagues. In a way, the reporting doctor takes on the role of his own patient, and the group becomes the doctor. They share his anxieties and may pick up what he has missed due to his blind spots...' (Gill 1985)

The group process does not teach skills or manoeuvres, but aims at a 'limited but considerable change' (Balint 1957) in the doctor's personality. It helps each participant to extend his range and methods of working by enabling him to use his own personal potential more fully. He gains additional understanding of his involvement with the patient and, over the years, gains a greater understanding of himself too.

There are many aspects of a doctor's work. It is the *integration* of these various elements and their appropriate use that is the aim of successful training. If the training results in a doctor who carries on his general practice regardless but performs what might be described as 'psychotherapy on Sundays', it has failed. And if it results in a doctor who becomes so interested in pursuing his patients' psyches that he persecutes them with inappropriate curiosity, e.g. 'How's your sex life?', and becomes dissatisfied and neglectful of the rest of his medical work, then again the training has failed. A successful marriage produces a new individual, not just a chip off one or other of the old parental blocks.

It is the leader's job to preserve the aims of the group and help it remain focussed on its primary task. Groups often prefer to do almost anything other than this. They take refuge by flight into other preoccupations and the leader has to watch out for these, steering a course between anecdotal chit-chat, journeys of psychological speculation into the patient's past, constant questioning of the presenting doctor or drowning him with 'helpful' advice, at the same time avoiding anything that might be too personal or painful for the doctor.

This method is both a technique for training, still remaining the principal one for training general practitioners in this sort of work, and a technique for research. For research it can be used to study the present state of play in the general practitioner's world, like a sampling net lowered at a particular point to chart the changes and developments that are occurring as the wider medical and social culture evolves. Some groups have also met to research particular aspects of their work, such as marital problems (Courtenay 1968), repeat prescriptions (Balint et al. 1970) or abortions (Tunnadine and Green 1978).

- **Developments**

An important change of emphasis and technique occurred in the 1970s. During the early years, the doctors tended to become semi-psychotherapists, devoting long sessions to their patients with psychological problems. This was an inevitable side-effect of the training and reflected the doctors' need to model themselves on the work of the leaders, a defence against the real difficulty of achieving an independent and appropriate professional identity for themselves.

The doctors' psychotherapeutic work had to become better integrated with their everyday work, making it less of a foreign body. New techniques had to be discovered to fit the general practitioner's timescale. A research group, again with the Balints' leadership, began meeting in 1965 to study this problem. They published their findings in a book called *Six Minutes for the Patient* (Balint and Novell 1973). The change in thinking that lay behind this work was as significant as the original work itself. They described the change from a history-taking style of interview, which they called the **detective inspector** approach, with the doctor conducting a search of the patient's life for significant events and feelings, to one in which the doctor listens intently to the patient's presentation, trying to tune in to how the patient wants to use the doctor and what this means. In this style of work more autonomy is left with the patient, who sets the pace, and the doctor has to be content to abandon his central role and follow the patient, being more aware of their relationship and less curious about secrets in the patient's inner world, or finding out what makes the patient tick. This is a more appropriate method for the brief encounters characteristic of general practice and leaves the patient's self-esteem intact. While working in this way **flash** interviews may occur, in which there is a sudden mutual awakening between doctor and patient with a consequent change in their relationship. 'Often the flash concerns the relationship between doctor and patient, but even if it does not, the relationship is changed by the flash' (Balint and Novell 1973). Relationships in general practice often seem to progress through these 'flashes' or 'important moments' (Gill 1985).

Balint had a considerable literary gift and used many metaphors which are still highly resonant. He described doctors as possessing an **apostolic function** by which he meant:

> '...the way in which every doctor demonstrates a vague but almost unshakeably firm idea of how a patient ought to behave when he is ill. Although this idea is anything but explicit and concrete, it is immensely powerful, and influences the way in which the doctor not only talks to the patient and relates to him, but how he prescribes drugs, and the way in which he expects to be treated by the patient. It is almost as if every doctor had a revealed knowledge of what is right and what is wrong for patients to expect to endure, and further, as if he had a sacred duty to convert to his faith all the ignorant and unbelieving amongst his patients' (Balint 1957).

A doctor's apostolic function is shaped mainly by his own personality and his personal attitudes to suffering and illness but it is also influenced by the social culture in which he lives. Every culture has powerful apostolic beliefs of its own about health, as well as other things, and these are changing all the time. The apostolic attitudes of thirty years ago may no longer be relevant now. In our world, we may expect people 'to work through their grief appropriately' or 'to take responsibility for their own health, not using alcohol, coffee or tablets but learning to meditate instead'. It is worth examining what is meant by such phrases and whose concerns they reflect: the patient's or the doctor's?

Balint also often referred to the doctor as the **drug doctor**, saying he was the most frequently used drug in medical practice and calling for further study of his uses and side-effects. Revealingly, it is the most frequently misquoted of Balint's aphorisms. Doctors usually describe the 'doctor' as 'the most powerful drug used in medical practice'! The apostolic function is alive and well.

General practice owes the Balints a debt of great gratitude. It is almost inconceivable to imagine people coming from positions of outside expertise, bringing the same painstaking willingness to study, listen and learn from the doctors as did the Balints, and not adopting a position of 'telling them what they ought to be doing' — an invitation only very exceptional people can refuse.

● **Wider Changes**

Since the 1950s, there have been many developments which have influenced general practice; vocational training has become firmly established, a Royal College of General Practitioners has been founded and departments for teaching general practice have been created in most medical schools. There has also been a rapid growth in the number of 'therapies' and 'techniques' of a broadly psychotherapeutic nature, and some of these have influenced psychotherapeutic work in general practice. Family therapy, counselling and the different approaches to sex therapy all contribute to the ways in which a general practitioner can choose to develop his style of work. They are like articles of clothing for the general practitioner to try on, taking something from this one and other things from another one, adding to his range of techniques and skills alongside those acquired through his medical training. He has to find out, though, how well they fit this particular setting and how well they fit his particular personality. None has yet been sufficiently studied from within the particular perspective of general practice.

● **Body and Mind**

The general practitioner has to try to achieve an jntegration in his work between those skills and attitudes that come from the more authoritarian traditions of the medical profession with those other quieter listening skills that come from the psychoanalytic tradition. When to ask questions and when to listen? He has to learn sufficient flexibility for the one to be part of the other.

A young man comes to the doctor, looking rather sleepy, and complains of a heavy chest, wondering whether it could be his 'heart'. The doctor can find nothing obviously wrong. The consultation seems lifeless, but in an aside which the doctor easily might have overlooked, the patient mentions that his father died a year ago. His father had been less than sixty when he died of a heart attack and father had been less than sixty when he died of a heart attack and his father's father had also died young, raising the question of a familial hyperlipidaemia. The patient expresses little grief and does not feel his father's death has affected his life much. He mentions that he now visits his mother more often and seems to resent this.

The doctor has to balance his medical responsibilities, such as defining the patient's lipid status and giving him necessary advice about this, while also noticing his own reactions and the patient's appearance and listening for clues to this young man's heavy heart. The patient seems depressed without knowing it, quite unconsciously bringing his complaint to the doctor. He does not seem to feel as much grief as the doctor first expects. But the doctor must allow the patient's own story to unfold, without superimposing his own expectations.

This is a typical brief encounter, where there is a balance between medicine and listening, both being part of each other, not an 'either/or'. The patient has had some limited but relevant help at a time when he presented himself for it. He may leave it there or return some time later. If he does come back, the first impressions have been laid, on both the doctor's and the patient's side.

The illness or health of an individual depends on a complex inter-relationship between the total person and his environment. Within the individual there is a constant interaction between the body, the mind with its powerful emotional world both conscious and unconscious, and whatever moral and spiritual life the person has and through which he relates his life to other people and the world at large.

The doctor has a relationship with the *whole person* and often with the whole of a family too. The body and the mind reflect and influence each other all the time. There is no such easy divide as people often make. The split between the two is a very common feature of illness, where a physical tension, an ache or a rash remain quite unconnected in the patient's mind to the conflicts that may be associated with them. Medical thinking is often also split in this way with physical illness being considered first, leaving the mind as a sort of remainder. The patient is put through a sieve marked physical in order to catch only those aspects that the doctor feels he understands and can do something about. The antagonism sometimes observed between medical consultants and psychiatrists is an expression of this divide, with the two seeming to inhabit different worlds and psychoanalysis, in isolating the mind for particular study, is also prone to accentuating this problem.

The general practitioner is uniquely placed for an understanding and healing of this relationship. He is working across the 'body/mind' boundary practically all the time. The whole spectrum of illness is brought to him, from the almost entirely physical to the almost entirely psychological. It reflects different densities of disturbance. At the most concrete end, serious physical illnesses like cancers and arterial disease always have important psychological consequences; in the middle range there are large numbers of illnesses in which body and mind seem to be inextricably bound up with each other, like asthma, the irritable bowel syndrome, hypertension, migraine and abnormalities of menstruation; and at the lighter end there are the transient physical expressions of tension — odd pains, headaches and autonomic symptoms that come according to personal patterns of anxiety and depression.

The doctor handles, touches and listens through his stethoscope while also keeping alert and listening through his human ear as well. He examines the body at the same time as noticing the patient's reactions to this process.

Not everything has to be verbalized. If psychological tensions are expressed, which had been close to the surface anyway, their physical counterparts may resolve as well, but such connections are most often quite inaccessible. The doctor must learn to mediate his medicine through whatever language, be it largely physical or largely psychological, that the patient is using at that time.

Mr. C. is a tall young banker in his late twenties, married to an attractive schoolteacher. They are expecting their first baby and Mrs. C. comes regularly for her antenatal care. She is rather jolly and seems pleased to be pregnant. The doctor has only seen the husband once or twice before and on this occasion Mr. C. seems rather more reserved than before and the two do not easily get on to the right track. He has been having intermittent diarrhoea and abdominal discomfort for some weeks. The doctor and patient fence around a bit but do not seem to get anywhere. Maybe this is the beginning of ulcerative colitis? The doctor sends him for some tests that all turn out to be normal. Mr. C. is still pretty unforthcoming when he comes again, but is perhaps a little keener for the doctor to get on to the right wavelength this time and drops more of a hint. He describes his symptoms as 'blowing out' and says he is 'almost as big as his wife'. The doctor senses an important area, makes some exploratory remarks, and when he is more sure of his footing says, 'You can look forward to the birth of babies but you can dread it too'. With doctor and patient now better tuned, the patient can express some of his feelings about the forthcoming baby: '... he hates babies, they puke and make a noise, the smaller they are the worse they are, he can't stand his friends' babies because he has seen how they have changed them, ruining their lives ...'.

The patient seems to resent the intrusion of the pregnancy and is frightened by the changes that it may produce. He fears they may have to move, as there will not be enough space for the baby (or for himself?) and nowhere to retreat in peace, as he is someone who dislikes displays of strong feelings. He is angry and fears the baby will change his life, leaving him left out of the relationship between the baby and his wife. It is possible that this strong feeling of the patient's was echoed in the doctor-patient relationship where he may have felt left out by the doctor and his wife, something that very often happens in antenatal care. Perhaps they had left him with an unfair amount of the negative resentful feelings attached to the forthcoming birth? The patient afterwards felt that both sides of his experience, positive and negative (for he was also looking forward to the birth), had been accepted by the doctor, making him feel less of an outcast. He had earlier described the baby as a 'monster'. It is also possible (and there was some evidence from later joint antenatal visits) that after this consultation, Mr. and Mrs. C. were able to communicate with each other about such an important change in their lives in a more open and balanced way.

Still within the psychosomatic sphere, the body may literally almost break under a psychological strain.

Mr. J. an earnest young man of twenty six, had been sent to his doctor by his employer because he had collapsed with back pain six weeks earlier and had still not fully recovered. The doctor had not seen him before but he gave the history of his back pain clearly. He was an only child who had always done well academically. He had 'passed everything' until recently failing some exams to become a solicitor. He had been working very hard to retake them and his parents had suggested he went away with them for a Bank Holiday weekend. He was pleased he went, but returned home earlier than his parents, in order to continue his studies. After he left, his mother had suddenly died. Normally, he would have phoned them on his safe arrival, but that night he did not. He was devastated. He had always found emotion less easy to share with his father and he adopted a role of 'carrying on', throwing himself into hard work, redoubling his efforts to do well in his retake exams. These he passed. As the pressure began to relax, only a few days later he 'collapsed' with back pain and was taken to a hospital casualty department, where he was sent home with analgesics and told to rest, advice which his firm's doctor had later repeated.

During the consultation described, in which this history emerged, the patient's emotions also emerged at the same time. He was able to break down in tears, particularly when reliving the bitter anguish he felt that his mother had not been able to share in his examination success. What had it all been for?

The patient had himself half-known that his back had cracked as a result of the tension and strain of his suppressed feelings after his mother's funeral. But he needed a doctor who could allow him to make the connection more confidently and who could help him express some of the full-hearted emotions which he had bottled up inside his body in order to carry on with his work.

'The helping him express' is often written about as 'allowing the patient to express'. It is more than that. It is the doctor experiencing some aspects of the patient's predicament and feelings, and giving them back through his words and reactions as a rightful experience for the patient to be having. It is a reinforced or positive echo returning to the patient from the doctor. The patient leaves feeling 'yes, that *is* what I feel'. His authenticity as an individual is strengthened. This is, of course, helpful only if the experience does have the feeling of *truth for the patient*. Otherwise, it may be that the feeling of conviction belongs more to the doctor's end. This is an ever-present danger.

● **Living in the Present**

Patients often apologise when they take the doctor's time. 'I'm sorry to take up your time (again?), doctor'; 'I won't keep you a moment, doctor'. Sentences which can carry many different emphases and meanings and which most often the doctor hardly notices. *The way* in which patients ask for the doctor's attention *matters*. Why does this patient always seem unsatisfied or unable to tolerate other patients in the waiting room? Why is this one over-apologetic and another anxiously over-friendly? *How* people present their problems to the doctor may reveal important patterns in their relationships and these may be closely related to their current difficulties. The doctor must allow such patterns to develop, being careful not to do so only to gratify his own needs, say, for patients to be appreciative or friendly. He may sense, when he is with a particular patient, that he is perceived as a parent who has to be appeased or a lover who must not come too close, an old friend or somebody the patient always has to do battle with but never completely defeat.

The doctor has to try and recognize, *there and then*, when one of these characteristic patterns of relating is being enacted with him and whether or not it is relevant. His listening must be efficient, hearing what is important at that moment.

A young woman in her thirties, Miss E., seems to the doctor prematurely grey and burdened. She has a likeable seriousness about her and is depressed. She had what she describes as a big emotional breakdown three years ago and has been depressed on and off since. She has a strong sense of duty and seems to live in a predominantly female world. She has a responsible job which she does very conscientiously, but feels that her supervisors do not take her work seriously enough. She is new to this doctor, who can feel how heavily depressed she is, but also how difficult it is for her to do anything with this, other than to endure it worthily. He is content to let her communicate in her own way and has to remain in the dark about many of the details of various relationships she hints at as current difficulties. If he does ask or enquire, he appears to add to her burden and she says, 'Oh, it would take such a long time, it's all so complicated anyway.

She comes seldom. On this occasion, she had not been for some time, but clearly had been very depressed. The doctor felt that he wanted her to realize that he was available for her as her doctor and finished the consultation by saying that she was able to come and see him if she felt depressed and that it was legitimate to make an appointment if she felt dreadful. It was not breaking any rules. At this point she conveyed that he had enough to deal with already and would not want to be burdened or spend more of his time seeing her. This was said genuinely, not evasively. She said it in such a way that she seemed to be making *herself* responsible for *his* burden. He pointed this out to her, suggesting that she had enough to carry already, without also having to worry about his decisions in allocating his time and energy. He would look after that himself.

The doctor could feel her conflict. It was not just that she did not want to burden him. If it had been, his remarks would have made no impact. It was that she desperately wanted to burden him, but also could not allow herself to do so, and that in part her depression was related to her habit of carrying other people's responsibilities as well as her own, a pattern perhaps originally established with her parents, but certainly persisting into the present as well.

This was a crystallizing point in the relationship and clearly meant something significant to her. It had arisen with the doctor, but it was important in her difficulties all round. The same or a similar point may often have come up, after all such a problem is not uncommon, but it seemed *particularly true* at that *particular moment* and was intimately related to the problems the patient was suffering in her current life. It has much of its impact for the patient because of the feelings contained in the doctor-patient encounter in which it is spoken.

Miss E. did return after quite a short interval and this time was able to talk to the doctor more about her distress, initiating a series of appointments with him at a time when she needed help.

It is worth noting that the doctor at this stage knows nothing about the patient's father, her mother or her siblings and very little of her present relationships. He does not know about her sex life, whether she has a boyfriend, a girlfriend or no friends. If he had asked her, he would have been unable to help her in the way he did. He had to be prepared to follow the patient, trying to make sense of whatever patterns emerged.

● **Time**

It is very often said that general practitioners do not have enough time to listen to their patients. This is far from the truth. The general practitioner's timescale is one of his setting's great strengths. He builds his knowledge of his patients and their families, through repeated short contacts, sometimes over many years. It is his use of the time that matters. His appointment system is flexible. He can see a patient for five minutes on one occasion, twenty minutes on another. He can see people frequently for a short time and then not need to again for months. Of course, if listening is simply a process of letting people talk, then indeed he does not have enough time. But it is not. It is the accuracy of attention to the moment that counts and an ear that 'hears' what is being said in the echoes and resonances behind the patient's words. No long preamble and fact finding is needed. The doctor and patient can get to the point quickly. Much of what is important will already be known.

> Mr. R. a widower in his sixties, seldom comes to the doctor, but does so one evening about two years after his wife's death. She had been a frequent attender whom the doctor knew well, an incessant talker with a great many complaints. Mr. R. is dressed in dull clothes, near Christmas, and comes with a 'croaky cold'. No time is needed for his own doctor who has known his whole situation over the years, to understand his croaky (tearful) cold (ness) and the lack of warmth he has felt in his life since his wife's death. The doctor gives him simple treatment for his cold and a few minutes of time, tears and some memories of the unexpectedness of her death, the shock …

This is all that is necessary. A brief consultation not necessarily requiring any follow-up.

For some patients the doctor remains one of the few fixed points. They may not come often, but know that he is there, as a reference point.

Most important is the patient's pattern of use over time. Is there a change? Is the patient coming more often or less often? One axis of the doctor's timescale is long-term, but the rhythm of use along the way can be very variable. This reflects the distance the patient may feel he needs at different times, sometimes coming to the doctor for quite intense help and then staying away. This pattern itself may have important echoes.

> Miss J. is a slim twenty-three-year-old student. She is a northerner and often comes to the surgery with a friend who stays in the waiting room. When she joined the doctor's list she came for a repeat prescription of her pill, a routine visit in which no problems were mentioned. She returned a month later to tell the doctor she was having a difficult time with sex with her present boyfriend. She felt dry and was put off by the thought of intercourse. She was shy and embarrassed with the doctor, but told him that she had known Robert for two years, that he had been prepared to build up their relationship slowly which had been important for her as she had easily felt pushed into bed by men previously. She had recently changed digs and so was new to the doctor's area, but felt her present 'home' would suit her better. She had felt tense with her past family and feared that someone might walk into her bedroom at any moment if she had her boyfriend there.
>
> The doctor and Miss J. managed to establish enough contact and Miss J. would come every few weeks, sometimes more often, sometimes less, to talk to the doctor and report on progress in her relationship with Robert. The doctor had suggested seeing them together as a couple and had discussed referring them for specialist psychosexual help. Neither of these suggestions had worked out. During this time she also talked a little about her family background and other relationships. Her mother and she were 'peas in a pod'. Her father, in fact her stepfather, had been very strict but she was his 'favourite'.

The doctor felt he had to be careful not to undermine the patient's relationship with Robert, hoping instead to help Miss J. become more receptive to him.

The doctor was careful to let her dictate the pattern and frequency of her attendance, as she had clearly signalled that this was important to her in her relations with men. She did not like to be pushed. It seemed to be the doctor's task to respect this aspect of her, but not too much. He had also to push her a bit as well, towards examining some of her reactions and possible reasons for them; gently steering a course between 'too much' and 'too little'. On one occasion the doctor finished an interview feeling he had probably overdone it and gone into things more deeply than was comfortable for the patient. However, on the next occasion she returned she looked more feminine and said she had a confession to make. They had successfully made love. On that occasion her friend had not accompanied her to the waiting room.

This kind of work tends to progress, then run into new difficulties — backwards and forwards. Miss J. seemed to keep attending when she wanted to and the doctor continued to try and balance his encouragement with allowing her to set the pace.

This work goes on amidst all the other demands that are made on a doctor's attention. He has many other difficult tasks to perform and his mind may often be far from being tuned in to his patients. The doctor will need to find a balance for himself between engaging and identifying with his patients on the one hand, and gaining sufficient distance from them on the other for thoughtful professional reflection. He will need both if he is to remain useful to his patients and neither become too defensive and distant or 'clinical', nor be too close to think clearly and see his patients from a different angle than the one from which they see themselves. He can then show respect for his patient's own way of living and treat the patient as another human being and not only as the bearer of a diagnosis for the doctor to discover.

I have isolated some aspects of the general practitioner's work in order to draw attention to the possibilities his setting offers for psychotherapeutic work of a certain kind. I hope that some of the characteristics of this work can be seen from the cases I have discussed, all taken from a general practitioner's everyday work; the doctor's relatively easy personal accessibility; his involvement with patients at times of need and change; his 'being there' for people (regardless of how often consulted) for long periods of time, often for many years; his relationship with the *whole* patient; the fact that the patient holds the key and can therefore dictate the pace, coming at a time of his own making (*Why now?* What is important to *this* patient at *this* time?); listening all round the patient as well as to echoes in himself; being content to do *just enough* and not more, so that the patient may leave feeling free to use the doctor at another time, or in a different way, without having to bear his soul more than he wants or having his life interpreted to him. The patient remains in charge of his own life and, hopefully, is strengthened and not undermined by his contact with the doctor.

● **References**

Balint M. (1954) Training General Practitioners in Psychotherapy. *Br. Med. J.* **1**, 115.

Balint M. (1955) The Doctor, His Patient and the Illness. *Lancet* **1**, 683.

Balint M. (1957) *The Doctor, His Patient and the Illness*. Pitman Medical, London.

Balint M., Hunt J., Joyce D. et al. (1970) *Treatment or Diagnosis: A Study of Repeat Prescriptions in General Practice*. Tavistock Publications, London.

Balint E. and Novell J. S. (eds.) (1973) *Six Minutes for the Patient*. Tavistock Publications, London.

Brown D. and Pedder J. (1979) *Introduction to Psychotherapy*. Tavistock Publications, London.

Collings J. S. (1950) General Practice in England Today: A Renaissance. *Lancet* **1**, 555.

Courtenay M. J. F. (1968) *Sexual Discord in Marriage*. Tavistock Publications, London.

Gill C. (1985) *Personal Communication*.

Goldberg D. P. and Blackwell B. (1970). Psychiatric Illness in General Practice. *Br. Med. J.* **1**, 439.

Hopkins P. (1956) Referrals in General Practice. *Br. Med. J.* **2**, 873.

Jarman B., Constantinidou M., Elder A. H. et al. (1985) *Personal Communication*.

Miller P. McC., Ingham J. B. and Davidson S. (1976) Life Events, Symptoms and Social Support. *J. of Psychosomatic Research* **20**, 515.

Prevention of Psychiatric Disorders in General Practice (1981). Report from General Practice 20, Royal College of General Practitioners, London.

Tunnadine D. and Green R. (1978) *Unwanted Pregnancy — Accident or Illness?* Oxford University Press, Oxford.

Winnicott D. W. (1972) *The Maturational Process and the Facilitating Environment*. (The International Psychoanalytical Library, No. 64) Hogarth Press, London.

6

Group psychotherapy

by Dick Blackwell

● **Introduction**
This chapter has six sections. The first provides an historical background, placing group psychotherapy in the context of the twin developments of sociological and psychological theories. Next is described the structure and process of psychotherapy groups, covering aspects of membership, duration, types of groups and how they function. The third section refers to the training of group psychotherapists, followed by a discussion as to how the group psychotherapy process is thought to work. The fifth section addresses the question of which patients to refer, while finally a look is taken at wider applications of group psychotherapy outside the purely clinical setting.

● **Historical Background**
The study of man and his relationship with his world has a long history, going back at least as far as the Ancient Greek philosophers over two thousand years ago. However, it was only in the nineteenth century that the discipline of sociology began to take shape and to formulate methods of studying whole societies scientifically. Durkheim, in his classic study of suicide, was one of the first to describe how individual behaviour can be understood as a function of social phenomena. Suicide, which had previously been understood as a most individual act, could now been seen as significantly influenced by social factors, that is by a person's relationship with others. Marx, too, argued that a person's whole being was essentially a function of his social relations. Although the precise ways in which social relationships influence individuals continue to be matters of further exploration and debate, the fundamental premise that man's social relationships are a crucial dimension of his well-being now seems firmly established.

The first third of the twentieth century saw the development, within sociology, of a concern not only with whole societies and classes which had been the focus of the nineteenth century pioneers, but also with interactions between small numbers of individuals. Sociologists such as Meade and Cooley began to study small social units and the way these influenced the individual's experience of himself. It was at this time that groups began to be used therapeutically.

Joseph Pratt began a group for tuberculosis patients in Boston in 1905, Edward Lazell in Washington treated schizophrenics in 1919, Trigant Burrow treated neurotics in 1920, Alfred Adler used groups generally in 1921, Julius Metzel worked with alcoholics, Cody Marsh used lecture and group discussion in New York in 1930, J. L. Moreno began psychodrama in the 1930s and Sam Slavson worked with disturbed children and subsequently established the idea of the small group whose structure and process provide the basis of much modern group psychotherapy. It is not clear how directly these pioneers were influenced by the sociological studies, but it is clear that both sociologists and group therapists were participating in the same trend towards an increased understanding of individuals in the context of their relationship with others.

This first third of the century also saw the development of psychoanalysis by Sigmund Freud and his colleagues. Freud was initially a clinician concerned with the treatment of individual patients but he rapidly became a major thinker about the nature and development of the human psyche in relation to its environment. Although he sought to apply his theories to the behaviour of small and large groups, and to whole societies, the individual remained the principle focus of his investigations through his psychoanalytic work. His theories of society were therefore based on his theories of the individual, whereas the sociologists proceeded in the opposite direction, to theories of the individual based on the study of groups and societies.

The last fifty years have seen an increasing integration of these two orientations, particularly in the theory and practice of work with small groups of between six and twelve people. This work shows four distinct strands of development: that of Kurt Lewin with training groups (T groups); the work of Wilfred Bion analysing the group as a single psychic unit; the investigations of Wolf and Schwartz doing psychoanalysis of individuals within the group setting; and particularly S. H. Foulkes who utilized the communication between group members as a therapeutic transaction.

Lewin emigrated from Germany during the rise of Nazism in the 1930s and settled in the USA. He conducted research on the effect of group membership on individuals and developed the theory of the social field in which each individual existed. This was derived from the concept of a force field in physics. His work was applied in organizations and used widely in management training programmes.

Bion was an English psychoanalyst working as an army psychiatrist when he began his work on groups. Based at the Northfield Military Hospital outside Birmingham, he addressed problems of group morale and was a key instigator of what became one of the first 'therapeutic communities'. He studied the group as a single unit and tried to develop group specific concepts. But, ultimately, he further explained these group concepts in terms of the psychoanalytic theories of Freud and Melanie Klein (the latter had significantly advanced psychoanalytic theory by applying it to the study and treatment of children). Bion thus produced a psychoanalytic theory of groups which has had considerable influence on the development of group psychotherapy in the UK. It has also been used, like Lewin's theory, in the understanding of organizations and in management training and consultancy.

Wolf and Schwartz were American psychoanalysts who developed a form of group therapy focussed on the individual. The group setting enabled them to observe the way each individual behaved in relation to the others. They could then comment on this individual behaviour and offer insights to each one in the traditional psychoanalytic way. They did not apply any particular theories of group behaviour. They regarded the group as a setting in which individual proclivities were revealed and exposed for analysis, rather than seeing group process in itself as an agent of change.

Foulkes was, like Lewin, an émigré from Nazi Germany, coming to England during the 1930s. In Germany he had been closely associated with the Frankfurt Institute for Social Research and his thinking was significantly influenced by the sociological work undertaken there. Like Bion, he worked at the Northfield Military Hospital and played a major part in the development of the 'therapeutic community' there. He was also a psychoanalyst who applied psychoanalytic concepts to the understanding of groups. But he saw the process of interaction *between* members of the group as the primary therapeutic process. The role of the group therapist was to facilitate, or in his word 'conduct' this process. His term 'conductor' to describe the group therapist's role was analogous to the conductor of an orchestra, in which the members of the orchestra make the music, in combination with each other, with the conductor enabling this process and interpreting the musical themes. He regarded the individual as an inherently social being and regarded symptoms as disorders of social interaction, inarticulate ways of communicating with others. His theories, along with those of Bion, constitute the major strands of group psychotherapy in the UK.

In addition to these four strands, five other developments are worthy of note. The first is the development of psychodrama by Moreno in the USA. This was concerned with creating dramatic scenarios, such as role plays and simulations which enabled individuals to experience and express emotions which had often been supressed or of which they were not normally aware. Psychodrama is now a growing therapeutic mode in this country and is sometimes combined with other approaches as well as being used in its own right. It was Moreno who introduced the term 'group therapy' in 1925.

Secondly, there has been the work of Gregory Bateson and his associates studying communication between people. Combining theories of psychoanalysis, anthropology, epistemology and biology, their work provided the theoretical underpinnings for the rapid growth of family therapy over the last twenty-five years. They, like Foulkes, saw symptoms as aspects or functions of interactional processes between people, specifically people in the intimate relationships of family life. Whereas Foulkes applied this orientation to work with 'stranger groups' — that is, groups of people who were not otherwise known to each other, family therapists developed techniques for working directly with those social networks in which symptoms were occurring.

Thirdly, there has been the growth of the encounter group movement, often associated with the West Coast of the USA, but widely known and employed throughout the Western World. Carl Rogers and Fritz Perls were both pioneers in this field. Lewin's T groups contributed to some of the developments in this area, which also includes the psychologist Abraham Maslow and the school of gestalt psychology among its influences. Encounter groups are concerned with promoting the honest and open expression of feelings between people; that is seen as an inherently healthy and growth enhancing process. Such groups have tended to receive a 'bad press' in more conventional psychotherapeutic quarters, but more detailed study reveals significant similarities between some types of encounter group and more conventional psychotherapy groups (Lieberman et al. 1973).

Fourthly, there is the therapeutic community movement. Tom Main, firstly at Northfield Military Hospital and subsequently at the Cassel Hospital in Surrey, and Maxwell Jones at the Henderson Hospital, also in Surrey, have been the major pioneers of this approach within the National Health Service. Other important contributions outside the NHS have come from Elly Jansen at the Richmond Fellowship, R. D. Laing at Kingsley Hall in East London and Joe Berke and Morton Schatzman at the Arbours Association in North London. Therapeutic communities mobilize the curative powers of the group on a twenty-four-hours-a-day basis. The patients, usually called members, residents or even guests, live together in hospital, hostel or other type of dwelling forming their own community. Each member plays an active part in the running of the community's affairs. The staff participate too and help to enable the ingredients of communal life, such as co-operating, competing, supporting, challenging, to become therapeutic processes.

Finally, one of the most recent developments, which is currently being pioneered by Pat de Maré, is the study of a large group. He has employed the large group, numbering from fifteen to forty members, in the treatment of individual patients. But he is also concerned with its development as a social phenomenon, believing that the capacity for people to engage in dialogue in such an arena not only has a civilizing effect on the individual (that is, developing qualities of citizenship in a participatory democracy), but can also have a humanizing effect on society.

The foregoing overview will have given some idea of the breadth of the field of group psychotherapy. As I am a group analyst, much of what I have to say will inevitably reflect that orientation and may not necessarily hold true for other styles of group therapy. However, much of it will be generally applicable to what I would call conventional group psychotherapy, that is group psychotherapy as practised generally within the NHS and in other settings, by practitioners with psychoanalytic or psychodynamic orientations and an awareness of the importance of social processes.

• Structure and Process of Psychotherapy Groups

Frequency and Duration

Groups usually meet once weekly, although twice weekly or fortnightly meetings are possible variations. They usually meet for one and a half hours and great importance is attached to prompt starts and finishes, though a therapist may occasionally allow a few extra minutes if he deems it necessary to achieve an appropriate ending to the session.

Membership

The group will usually have between five and nine members, selected by the therapist to achieve a suitable mixture for the purposes of the group. In some groups all the patients will have been brought together because they have the same problem, for example alcoholism, drug addiction, sexual dysfunction, school refusal, etc. Alternatively, they may have an assortment of different problems. Likewise, with regard to age and gender, a group may be all of one sex or mixed; it may contain a very narrow age band, e.g. sufferers from mid-life crises, or have a wide spread from 20 to 65. It is preferable, however, to aim for balance in that no-one feels themselves to be 'out on a limb'. If the group contains both sexes, it is best to have as near as possible an equal number of each sex. If there is not to be just one problem represented, then there should be a good assortment. Five alcoholics, a depressive and someone with sexual difficulties would be unlikely to provide a useful mix. Neither is it a good idea to have one member much older or much younger than the rest. In short, the group should either be fully homogeneous along any particular dimension, or fully heterogeneous.

Opinions vary regarding the relative merits of hetero- versus homo-geneous groupings. It is argued, on the one hand, that patients get early comfort and support from others with whom they have much in common. This, along with the reassurance that they are not alone in their predicament can speed the early phases of the group's development and may also lead to more enduring understanding and intimacy which will promote the therapeutic process. On the other hand, such a group may lack the variety, difference in perspective and, therefore, new information that is available in heterogeneous groups. Homogeneous groups may share common blind spots and will have only the therapist to challenge them.

Co-therapy

There is usually just one therapist to each group except where there are specific reasons for having two people working as co-therapists. Couples' groups, where marital or cohabiting partners come together with other couples, is an example in which co-therapy is widely used. Co-therapy may also be helpful for inexperienced therapists, either learning by partnering a more experienced colleague or working with another inexperienced colleague for mutual support and confidence. Co-therapy can also provide valuable learning for experienced therapists who may be put 'on their mettle' by the presence of a potentially critical colleague. At the same time, they may find the presence of a colleague provides them with the security to be more adventurous as therapists. It is also likely that groups that have no special reason for requiring it can nevertheless benefit considerably from the input of two therapists instead of one. On the other hand, co-therapists need to be able to play together like tennis partners and if they cannot harmonize their input and resolve their own inevitable differences, they will considerably handicap the group.

Closed and Open Groups

Closed groups run for a fixed period of time with the same members. They may meet for as few as six or twelve sessions, or they may continue for a year or more. New members do not join during the course of the group, even if one or more of the original members drop out.

Open groups do take in new members as others leave and usually have no fixed time period. They may continue for many years, during which time they will completely renew their membership. Patients remain in these groups for varied periods. From eighteen months to two years is usually regarded as a minimum period for full benefit to be derived from the group. However, some patients may stay for over five years, not necessarily in order to resolve their initial difficulty but often because they continue to derive other benefits from being in the group.

Group Process

When they meet, the group members sit in a circle with the therapist or therapists.* They will usually stay in their seats for the whole meeting since the process is essentially one of verbal and visual communication. The therapist will not generally ask them to change places, move about or touch each other, nor will he expect them to do so spontaneously. Inevitably, however, there will be times when one member will extend a comforting hand to another in distress and the therapist is unlikely to regard this as against the rules. There are a few conventional group psychotherapists who will, from time to time, incorporate psychodrama techniques into group therapy and would then have their patients moving about accordingly.

There is no formal agenda for group discussion and the therapist will not initially offer any direction. He will leave the group to talk about anything they want to bring up and to get to know each other in whatever way they choose. The therapist will allow this process to develop, watching and listening, and will then contribute in his own way to enable the group members to learn from their own experience of the process in which they are participating. The sort of interventions the therapist makes will depend on his own personal style and on his theoretical orientation.

Among the possible contributions of the therapist are the following: questioning of either the whole group or individuals to elicit information or to encourage further thought and exploration of a particular issue, e.g. 'How old were you when your father died?'; 'How do you feel about what M has just said?'; disagreeing with a particular statement made or a position taken by a group member, e.g. 'I disagree with your view that sex should not be discussed in the group'; drawing attention to aspects of group or individual behaviour which have not been noticed by the participants, e.g. 'I notice that every time A and B get angry with each other, J clutches the arms of his chair very tightly'; 'Every time P brings up his jealousy, someone else quickly changes the subject'; interpretation of unconscious themes, e.g. 'You have talked a lot about competition in your jobs, I think you are also referring to the competition here in the group'. Sometimes the group will lapse into silence. At such times, the therapist will usually wait with the group until the conversation is resumed. He will only break the silence if he feels he has something particular to say at that point. He will not see it as his responsibility to keep the conversation going.

•   Training of Group Psychotherapists

It is generally agreed that group therapists need to have their own experience of receiving therapy. They must know themselves and how they

---

*The rest of this explanation will assume only one therapist.

respond to others, and how others respond to them. Some schools of thought would regard individual therapy as an adequate preparation for a trainee therapist, while others would insist on experience as a patient in a group. The Institute of Group Analysis requires its trainees to spend at least three years as patients in an analytic group.

In addition to having therapy themselves, trainees will study one or more of the theories of group process and of problem or symptom formation and resolution. They will usually spend two years conducting one or more groups under supervision. This supervision may involve meeting individually with a supervisor to report on and discuss the group but, more usually, it will involve meeting with other trainees in a group led by the supervisor. The supervisory process will then reflect certain important dimensions of the therapeutic process.

● **How does Group Psychotherapy Work?**

There are a number of theories about how group psychotherapy works. These cover different views about how symptoms and problems arise and how they are resolved.

In the traditional psychoanalytic view, symptoms are manifestations of internal conflicts in the unconscious part of the individual's mind. These conflicts date back to infancy when ideas, wishes, desires and accompanying fears were 'repressed' from consciousness. This repression results from social prohibitions such as the incest taboo or from fantasies such as the male child's fear of being castrated for having incestuous desires. In psychoanalytic psychotherapy the patient re-enacts the infant-parent relationship in the patient-therapist relationship. The patient is said to 'regress' to the infantile state and to transfer on to the therapist the feelings that the infant had for his parents. In this way the repressed ideas, wishes, desires and fears begin to manifest themselves. The therapist draws the patient's attention to them so that they can become conscious, be expressed verbally and 'worked through'.

In a psychotherapy group these unconscious features of the infant-parent relationship become transferred on to other group members as well as to the therapist and even the group itself may be experienced as if it were a parent, usually the mother. Group members may also represent siblings for each other.

Other theories lay more emphasis on present conflicts and difficulties, and de Maré has introduced the term 'transposition' to describe the way in which a patient treats other group members not as figures from the past (infancy) but as figures from the present — spouses, lovers, friends, colleagues, enemies, rivals, etc. In this view, whole constellations of relationships can be transposed and re-enacted within the group. In this way, patients can become more aware of how they deal with problems in relationships with others and can experiment in the group setting with different ways of relating.

This view sees problems and symptoms arising in an individual's relationships with others. The headache which repels unwelcome sexual advances is an example which has entered contemporary folklore. In a group setting, sufferers from these headaches may learn to say 'no' more directly when not wishing to comply with another's wishes. Or in those cases where no does not just mean no, but is also an expression of feelings of anger, sadness, resentment or fear, a patient may also learn to recognize these feelings and express them more directly.

Irving Yalom has developed the following list of 'curative factors' which operate in groups: installation of hope, universality (the discovery of being like everyone else), imparting of information, altruism, corrective recapitulation of the primary group, development of socializing techniques, imitative behaviour, interpersonal learning, group cohesiveness and catharsis. He regards these as all interlinked in the dynamic process of the group.

Skynner has attempted to connect historical factors of infantile relationships in the family of origin with contemporary relationship difficulties. He suggests that the individual grows up in a family in which certain aspects of emotional life are avoided. These may be anger, jealousy, rivalry, intimacy, sadness, sexuality, etc. The individual's repertoire of behaviour and communication is consequently limited by growing up in this context. Furthermore, he evolves a philosophy of life, chooses friends and enemies, jobs and pastimes, lovers and spouses in accordance with this limited repertoire. In turn, as a parent, he will influence the development of his children in a similar way. If at any point the individual encounters a situation for which his existing repertoire has no satisfactory response, he will encounter an apparently insoluble problem or develop a symptom which brings him to therapy. Because of the diversity and variety of interaction in a therapy group, the patient is likely to encounter the very situation that was avoided in his family and which the patient has successfully avoided prior to the occurrence of the problem or symptom presented for therapy. In the group, the patient has to deal with the situation and experience the avoided emotion. It is only after he has done this that he is able to have insight and look back on his previous pattern of avoidance. This theory is particularly interesting in that it describes a scenario of change which need not necessarily be confined to the therapy situation. Such challenges to a person's habitual ways of relating, which were learned in the family of origin, can occur in other areas of life where they cannot be avoided. Thus, psychotherapy is not the only arena in which change and growth takes place. This is in contrast to more traditional psychoanalytic theories which suggest that such change and growth can be achieved only through regression and interpretation of infantile conflicts in the psychotherapeutic setting.

Foulkes regarded symptoms as forms of communication. They were the result of disorders in the social network of the individual patient who became the locus for the expression of the disorder. Foulkes regarded the group process as essentially one of communication in which symptoms can be seen to be 'inarticulate' ways of communicating. Through the therapy group process, the individual can learn to communicate more satisfactorily. He will then be able to improve the patterns of communication within his social network, which were the source of the original symptom. Foulkes developed the concept of the group matrix to describe the complex 'transpersonal' network of communication which emerges in a group. As was noted in the historical background, his view has marked similarities to that of Bateson and the family therapy tradition. Bateson also regarded symptoms as arising from communication patterns in social networks, particularly families, so that changed communication would be the therapeutic goal. He focussed on 'levels' of communication and learning and applied the theory of logical types developed by the philosophers Russell and Whitehead. This resulted in the famous double bind theory of schizophrenia. But perhaps because this focus was so specifically on families, his theories are widely applied in family therapy but not as yet in group therapy.

●   **Who to Refer for Group Psychotherapy**

Again, there is diversity of opinion on this subject. Some therapists have very clear ideas on which diagnostic categories can be helped by group therapy and which cannot. However, Rutan and Stone point out that 'most exclusionary recommendations in the literature can be countered by other published recommendations that such patients are treatable in groups'. There is also disagreement as to whether traditional psychiatric or even psychoanalytic diagnostic categories are actually useful in deciding on a patient's suitability for a group. It is my view that these categories are not very useful, because the success of therapy depends much more on how a particular patient 'gets on' with a particular therapist. Such matching is quite idiosyncratic.

The classification of patients in whatever diagnostic terms can provide only crude guidelines. What is really valuable is for medical practitioners to make personal contact with the psychotherapists to whom they might refer patients for psychotherapy. Obviously, there are limitations to this but, as a general guideline, the better a referrer knows the therapist, the more able he will be to make appropriate referrals. A discussion between practitioner and therapist about the *possibility* of referring a particular patient for therapy is in my view invaluable to all concerned, and such preliminary pre-referral discussions will also offer doctor and therapist an opportunity to make contact.

Medical students with whom I have discussed this seem to feel it is incumbent on them to decide whether or not a patient should be referred for therapy. As doctors already have to carry a great deal of responsibility, there seems no good reason for expecting them to carry this additional and unnecessary burden which should more appropriately be shared with their psychotherapist colleagues.

The therapist assessing a patient for a group is concerned not only with how he gets on with the patient, but also with how the patient will relate to other members of the group. Apart from being concerned with having a balanced group in terms of age, sex and other dimensions described in the section on group composition, the therapist will also have an intuitive sense of how certain patients might relate to each other. However, despite this need for each group therapist to consider each referral on its own merits, it is possible to make some tentative generalizations to aid referrers, both in terms of who might benefit and who might not.

Clearly, the major criterion must be the view that a particular symptom is amenable to psychological treatment. Many illnesses previously regarded as purely physical are now thought to have a significant psychological component. Medical practitioners themselves will differ in the extent to which they regard such ailments as tuberculosis, cancer, asthma, pre-menstrual tension, allergies, etc. as suitable for psychological as well as physical treatment. It is also important that the patient himself is prepared to seek psychological help. A patient convinced, despite his doctor's opinion, that there is no psychological component in his complaint is likely to enter a therapy group with the intention of failing to improve in order to demonstrate the irrelevance of group therapy to his particular problem. Such an attitude suggests a poor prognosis.

This willingness of the patient to try to use group therapy positively applies equally, if more obviously, with psychological symptoms. Whilst the value of group therapy may be obvious to the doctor and psychotherapist, it may not necessarily be obvious to the patient. It is important to distinguish between the patient who is anxious and uncertain about trying something new, but will respond to encouragement and explanation, and the patient who is just not willing to make the investment of time and energy necessary to benefit from group therapy. The former may have a good chance of benefitting from it, the latter is virtually assured of failure.

As well as the type of unmotivated patient described above, there are some other contra-indications. One of these is a lack of impulse control, such that the safety of other group members is at risk. Another is an immediate crisis requiring immediate help, with no time to enter a group and establish relationships which can lead to change. Having a speech impediment or other difficulties with language sufficient to inhibit ordinary conversation are also contra-indications. In short, if a patient is able and willing to join a group and to participate in its process as outlined above, he has the possibility of benefitting from it. Anything that prevents this process from taking place can be deemed a contra-indication.

• Wider Application of Group Psychotherapy

As I indicated in the description of the historical development of group psychotherapy, its theories and techniques have not been confined to the field of psychiatry. Group therapy approaches are now commonly used, albeit in modified forms, in education, industry and with staff groups in both health and social services. Usually, the aim of such applications is to facilitate more open and effective communication between groups of people working together. It also provides an opportunity for discussion and sharing of the stresses and strains affecting both individuals and groups in their work setting. In education, Abercrombie has pioneered the use of group approaches to teaching university students. She adopted a group psychotherapeutic approach to create a non-authoritarian climate in seminars which enabled students to learn actively through discussion with each other, rather than passively by being given information and knowledge by the tutor.

Skynner worked with the staff of a comprehensive school. They met as a group to discuss the difficulties they had with the pupils. This resulted in a substantial decrease in the number of referrals from the school to the local child guidance clinic.

Groups are also used for training staff. The emphasis here is not on the functioning of a work group but on the individual development of the members. These groups may be used on management training courses where the participants do not share the same work setting. It is thought that the understanding of themselves and others that participants gain from the group experience will enable them to function more effectively in their jobs.

These developments are not yet as extensive as they might be. They are still only the beginnings of the extending of knowledge gained in psychotherapy to other areas of life, and extending the knowledge gained in those other areas back into psychotherapy. They are also beginnings in understanding the common dimensions of therapy, education, personal development and social change.

● **References**

Abercrombie M. L. J. and Terry P. M. (1978) *Talking to learn: Improving teaching and learning in small groups*. Society for Research in Higher Education, University of Surrey, Guildford.

Bateson G. (1972) *Steps to an Ecology of Mind*. Ballantine, New York.

Bion W. R. (1961) *Experience in Groups*. Tavistock Publications, London.

de Board R. (1978) *The Psychoanalysis of Organisations*. Tavistock Publications, London.

de Maré P. B. (1985) Large Group Perspectives. *Group Analysis,* **18**:2.

Foulkes S. H. (1948) *Introduction to Group Analytic Psychotherapy*. Heinemann, London.

Jansen E. (1980) *The Therapeutic Community*. Croom Helm, London.

Jones M. (1953) *The Therapeutic Community*. Basic Books, New York.

Lewin K. (1952) Defining the Field at a Given Time. In D. Cartwright (ed.), *Field Theory in Social Sciences*. Basic Books, New York.

Lieberman M. A., Yalom I. D. and Miles M. B. (1973) *Encounter Groups: First Facts*. Basic Books, New York.

Main T. F. (1946) The Hospital as a Therapeutic Institution. *Bulletin of the Menninger Clinic,* **10**:66.

Maslow A. (1968) *Toward a Psychology of Being*. D. Van Nostrand, New York.

Perls F. S. (1971) *Gestalt Therapy Verbatim*. Bantam, New York.

Rogers C. (1970) *Carl Rogers on Encounter Groups*. Harper & Row, New York.

Rutan J. S. and Stone W. N. (1984) *Psychodynamic Group Psychotherapy*. Collamore Press, Lexington.

Skynner A. C. R. (1983) Group Analysis and Family Therapy. *Int. of Grp. Psychother*. 34.

Wolf A. and Schwartz E. K. (1965) *Psychoanalysis in Groups*. Grune & Stratton, New York.

Yalom I. D. (1970) *The Theory and Practice of Group Psychotherapy*. Basic Books, New York.

7

Therapy, the family, and others

by Alan Cooklin

Individual psychotherapies, whether based on a model of learning theory or on psychodynamic understanding, have one thing in common. They view the patient from the standpoint that he or she is an integrated discreet organism. Family and other 'systems' therapies view the patient as one component in a system or 'organism' (e.g. the family) which may manifest its malfunction through the behaviour of that component — the patient. That is the major difference.

The purpose of this chapter is to elaborate that difference, the thinking behind it, some of the evidence which supports that thinking, and implications for intervention. The goal is that the practitioner should be stimulated to think of alternative ways to use his or her professional skill, in order to promote healthy changes in families and other human systems. It is not a chapter on 'How to be a family therapist' nor on 'What family therapists do'. Its aim is to offer the practitioner a broader view of the context of human psychological distress and thus to broaden the range of therapeutic options in the practitioner's repertoire.

To this end, the chapter will be organized in fourteen sections:

1. What is family therapy, both as a treatment and as a framework of conceptualization?
2. The family interactional model of psychiatry in relation to other models.
3. Theories of organization and interaction in families.
4. Family patterns and the 'family dance'.
5. Short-term patterns and patterns over time.
6. Balance and stability versus change in the family.
7. The question of intervention — does it work? Is it worth it? What are the dangers?
8. Some aspects of family therapy — how it operates.
9. Clinical example.
10. Various methods of therapy with the family.
11. Family therapy. Comparison of principles with individual psychotherapy and group psychotherapy.
12. Applications to different kinds of family structure and to 'non family' human systems.
13. What can the practitioner do?
14. Further reading and opportunities for learning and training.

- ## 1. What is Family Therapy?

Family therapy refers on the one hand to a 'treatment': an activity whereby a therapist sits down for one or more sessions with various members of a family to help them change something, and on the other hand to a framework for conceptualization, a way of understanding and thinking about human behaviour which may then be used in a variety of ways. This thinking may be applied to the family or to other contexts in which human beings live in proximity and may develop intimate relationships.

Two important components of the thinking are:

a. That people are not islands, and their behaviour can only be understood in the context in which it occurs. Thus the idea of a person having an 'internal' world is different from considering the individual in isolation. The internal world is no longer a 'closed shop', viewed only through the portal of dreams and other channels of the unconscious, but is accessible through the day-to-day interactions with others. These interactions themselves are then dependent on the context in which they occur. Consider the behaviour of a young mother towards an infant. If one takes the 'individual' perspective to absurd extremes, one could see the mother's behaviour principally in terms of her unconscious fantasies about the child, or her learned responses. Alternatively, one could recognize that the mother's behaviour will be affected by many factors. In some Indian cultures she would expect the child to be in almost constant physical contact with her for the first year or so of life, whilst in many Western milieux she might expect to have longish periods of separation from the child very soon after birth. Her responsiveness, and its degree of flexibility or rigidity, the degree of playfulness, anxiety, attentiveness or 'over-attentiveness' will also be affected by the child's response to her. If she perceives herself as looking after the child in a relatively hostile environment, she may be highly protective of every aspect of her child's life. In the first few weeks or months of life, this will give the child the freedom to develop. However, the context changes with time. The same behaviour on the mother's part when the child reaches 2, 3, 4 or 5 years of age may have the effect of no longer being protective but of becoming restrictive. The mother's and, therefore, the child's behaviour will also be heavily influenced by their relationships with others in their environment. For example, if the mother feels well supported by her husband, she will be less likely to perceive the environment as hostile and therefore be less liable to protect the child inappropriately. On the other hand, if her parents are seen as in competition with her husband, or if his family are seen as in competition with hers, the mother may be encouraged to isolate herself further, with her child as a mutual protection. These factors will have a major impact on an only child whilst, if there are many siblings, the effect will be diluted.

b. A second component of this thinking is that people in close physical and emotional proximity readily set up stable patterns of interaction. These patterns are made up from a whole series of sequences; repetitive short events involving two or more people. This will be elaborated in Section 4 entitled *Family dance*. The family presents a problem, either as an individual's symptom or behaviour, or as a set of 'problem' relationships. Then it is assumed that this problem is a manifestation of the total organization of the family. It is not so much that the family 'causes' the problem, but rather that the problem, as it develops, is part of the life and context of the family and can soon become part of what is familiar and comforting. A practitioner who does 'family therapy' will, therefore, be concerned with the total family organization and how this relates to the problem, rather than to any one individual. To do this he may use various methods, may work through individuals, but keeping his sights on the whole organism of the family. He may work with parts of the family, with the whole nuclear family or with the nuclear family and extended family of three generations or more. The therapy may last for one, two or many sessions of one or more hours. The commonest is for the therapist to work for a fairly small number of sessions, averaging about ten.

● **2. The Family Interactional Mode of Psychiatry in Relation to other Models**

Although psychiatry is a branch of medicine, to operate rationally it has to link all levels of human experience, physical, cognitive, perceptual, emotional and, in certain circumstances, philosophical and theological. It is therefore not surprising that, in the struggle to achieve some coherence, there has been much controversy about the correct focus for the subject. The proponents of these different views inevitably communicate a different kind of relationship with the patients who seek, or are brought for, their help (Cooklin 1973). The family interactional model implies not only a different relationship to include others, but might be expressed as: 'You present me with distress or disturbance. I see this disturbance as representing a problem in the organization of which you are a part, the family. Therefore, I will not respond directly to you: rather, I shall attempt to examine and change the organization of the family in the belief that this will also be of most benefit to you.'

The family interactional model is, therefore, concerned with the patient as part of a group, rather than just the relationship between patient and practitioner. It also differs in the way in which it approaches causality: the family interactional model does not imply that the family is noxious and has 'made the patient ill'. Rather, it is concerned with the way in which a number of factors, particularly the family organization and the interactional pattern in the family, have allowed part of the patient's behaviour to be congruent to the family's way of living, whilst another part of the behaviour remains incongruent. Consider a young anorectic girl in a family where the members have been used to being close and physically intimate with each other, in which conflicts have usually been kept at a low ebb and in which unity of the family has been valued highly. The girl's behaviour is discordant to the family in that she arouses much anxiety and, in such a family, feeding may have been highly valued. On the other hand, it may be congruent to the family in that her sexual development is delayed, she will take less interest in and be less attractive to boys, thus avoiding conflicts common in most families. She will stay at home closely involved with her family and her behaviour will keep other members of the family closely involved with her. One approach to the problem would be to consider the implications of the family adapting to a growing adolescent girl, to consider how the conflicts which would arise could be handled differently by her and the family. Such an approach would be addressing principally the organization of the family.

● **3. Theories of Organization and Interaction in Families**
Two related sets of ideas have provided frameworks for considering the family as a system rather than just a set of individuals. These are General Systems Theory and Cybernetics (Von Bertalanffy 1968, Ashby 1956).

General Systems Theory
General systems theory is not a theory of causality, but a theory of organization. It is a way of categorizing systems throughout nature both living and inanimate. It considers the family as a living system and considers its capacity to adapt in terms of:

a.   The boundary around the family and around the sub-systems in the family
This relates to the degree to which family members maintain a close unity within the family, or engage actively with the outside world. This, in turn, controls the input and output of information to and from the family. Information includes people. Thus a family with a very impermeable boundary will be likely to adapt poorly to the arrival of new members — babies, grandparents, boy or girl friends — and will be intolerant of members moving out (such as around the time of adolescence).

b.   The theory also considers the differentiation of the sub-systems within the family and the degree to which the boundary around these is clear
For example, the marital relationship is a separate sub-system from, say, the parental sub-system. In a family in which the members say 'we always do everything together' the differentiation of the parents having a separate relationship may be poorly recognized. This in turn may militate against the development of any other set of separate relationships.

c.   Supra systems and sub-systems
In addition to the degree to which the family is differentiated into sub-systems, it will also form part of other supra systems to varying degrees. For example, the family may be part of an extended family network and the different members may be part of other supra systems within the community — work, school, social groups etc.

Cybernetics
Cybernetics is a set of principles adapted from electronic control systems. The thermostat in a central heating system is the simplest example. Cybernetic principles are used to consider ways in which the family has developed habits which tend to neutralize or stabilize any change. In the example of the anorectic girl, the father became depressed after his daughter was admitted to hospital and

began to improve. Strains in the marriage appeared and the mother developed a number of hypochondriacal symptoms. The youngest sibling began to steal. The girl eventually became so worried about them all that she discharged herself from hospital and soon after resumed her fasting behaviour. The others then improved.

Thus, one could see the behaviour of the members of the family as responding to a change (the young girl leaving home) whilst the effect of their behaviour was ultimately to maintain stability, albeit an inappropriate stability and at a high cost. It was from observations such as these that the term 'family homeostasis' was coined (Jackson 1957).

• 4. Family Patterns and the 'Family Dance'

Imagine an event where you are sitting at dinner with some members of your family, say your parents if they are alive, or perhaps your children. Maybe there are others: grandparents, siblings, aunts, uncles or cousins. Imagine that a small and common or familiar conflict develops. Perhaps it starts with the question of who is to visit whom at the weekend, or some comment on your dress or diet. If you can imagine such a scene, you may be able to predict more or less accurately who would say what, roughly in what order, and the sort of tone with which each would speak. You may be able to go further. You may be able to predict to what degree of tension or passion the conflict will develop and two or three ways in which it will 'end'. What you will have remembered is an interactional sequence and one which is likely to be repeated with a similar shape and similar attitudes taken by the various members, despite the fact that the subject of conflict might differ markedly. I put the 'end' in inverted commas because, of course, it is not really the end. It is only the punctuation of a sequence which, together with other sequences, makes up the interactional pattern of the family. This sequence could 'end' with a senior member of the household perhaps looking stern, raising his voice, perhaps shouting, banging the table, perhaps threatening violence or perhaps carrying out violence. The amount of feeling and the level of conflict tolerated in different families will be idiosyncratic to that family. However, the ending of a sequence with one member taking a strong and challenging position is one pattern which will occur in many families.

There are many alternative punctuations to such a sequence. It could end with somebody becoming upset, bursting into tears, leaving the room or the house, or with another member placating and 'calming things down'. It could end with a diversion: someone making a joke, an external intrusion such as the telephone or perhaps a child becoming excited or misbehaving. Diversion by a child is a common ending to such a sequence of conflict in many families. In some families, however, the child's over-reaction to increasing tension is in somatic form. If the child has a predisposition to asthma for example, the child is likely to have an asthma attack at times of high tension, particularly if this concerns the parents. Such an attack will often then divert attention from the conflict in the family, as members of the family co-operate to assist the afflicted member (Minuchin 1978). At this point, one can see the problem of considering causality. One could say that the tension in the family precipitates the asthmatic attacks;

alternatively, one could say that the asthmatic attacks control tension in the family.

- ### 5. Short-term Pattern and Pattern Over Time

If you were able to imagine a family sequence, then you could ask, 'Who made it happen?'. The answer has to be, 'Everyone present'. In fact, if the sequence was experienced as unpleasant, most members of the family would probably admit that they had individually resolved 'never to let it happen like that again.' Yet as soon as they are together, they will often repeat a similar set of sequences.

The kind of sequence which I hope you have been able to illustrate from your own experience might repeat many times over the course of a few hours or days. To refer to the family of the anorectic girl, a common sequence would be that Susan would return from school and suggest to her mother that she was going out. The mother would complain that she did not help in the house but not directly insist that Susan stay in. As tension developed between the mother and Susan, younger brother Ben would demonstrate his 'difference' from Susan by offering to help his mother and telling her many things about his school day. Susan would become increasingly angry and provocative in response to Ben's relationship with his mother, to the point where, on father's return, the mother would make demands on him to control Susan. Conflict would then escalate between mother and Susan which would be followed by the parents arguing with each other. The children would then fight and the parents would then interrupt their own argument to control the two children. This is quite a complicated sequence. In various similar forms it would repeat frequently, and one could see how the girl's symptom of not eating could easily take the place of the children's fighting, in interfering with the parents' arguments, albeit arguments which they might see as having been 'caused' by her.

However, there are more complex patterns which repeat much less frequently. For example, in some families, one can observe that the mother and Susan remain on good terms, with father left out for approximately two to three months; perhaps this reverses, with father and Susan being close for a few weeks, after which mother and Susan are again close. The people in such a family know that each change is not really a 'change', but only a punctuation. There are perhaps also other sequences which repeat with much less frequency. One can often note that a particular set of behaviours occurs in one generation, misses a generation and then can be found between parents and child in the following generation.

The important point is that these patterns do not occur because somebody 'makes' them happen. Rather, they are a function of the organization of relationships which has become set up in the family. One could postulate unconscious motives for each member which propagate such patterns, but an important aspect of these patterns is that *they provide the family with some stability*. Inasmuch as maintaining stability is often experienced by the members as a way of protecting the family and those in it, therefore, one function of such behaviour is to achieve a degree of *mutual protectiveness*.

● **6. Balance and Stability Versus Change in the Family**

The family is a context in which people live. These people are at different levels of development, physically and emotionally. For this development to progress, a certain degree of stability is necessary. At the same time, a certain degree of flexibility is necessary for the family to adapt, for example, to the children requiring more independence, privacy, autonomy, etc. Thus, throughout all families, there is a constant tension between these contradictory forces for change and stability. Many problems can be understood in terms of the failure to resolve this conflict in the family.

In the family of the anorectic girl, the various behaviours of the family members could be seen as accommodating to the change in such a way as to temporarily maintain the previous status quo. Several research projects, e.g. Mossige (1979), have demonstrated that in families with a schizophrenic member there is a greater tendency, particularly in the case of the symptomatic member, for the individual opinions and perceptions to be modified to fit the 'orthodox family' opinion.

The work at the Philadelphia Child Guidance Clinic on what they term 'psychosomatic families' strongly supports the view that the illness in the child plays an important role in the regulation of conflict within the family. Their most dramatic study was to measure the free fatty acid level (FFA) of severely labile diabetic children and their parents during a standardized task interview (Minuchin op. cit.). The free fatty acid has been shown to rise in ketoacidosis, but is also a useful measure of emotional stress. The 'labile group' of diabetic children were requiring hospitalization for correction of acidosis as much as once a week. The child was initially left outside the room observing from behind a one-way mirror a family argument which the parents had been asked to solve. During this period, the free fatty acid in at least one of the parents would rise markedly while the level in the child would continue to rise slowly. The child was then brought into the room and the three of them were asked to help each other to resolve the argument. At this point the free fatty acid level in the parents markedly dropped while FFA in the child continued to rise more steeply, and it remained high after the end of the interview. Thus it would appear that the child's intervention actually lowered the level of stress in the parents.

● **7. The Question of Intervention**

Despite the plethora of research, there are but few controlled trials which successfully demonstrate the therapeutic efficacy of family therapy compared to other treatments. The best review of these is in the *Handbook of Family Therapy* by Gurman and Kinskarn (1981). In the 'labile diabetics' referred to earlier, the re-hospitalization rate dropped to almost nil after between three and twelve months' family therapy. Some very important work has been done by Leff and others (1982) which has conclusively demonstrated that the factor, 'expressed emotion', assessed in the relatives of schizophrenics can be a critical factor in forecasting the relapse rate of the patient. When the expressed emotion is high, the relapse rate may be over 90 per cent regardless of the drug therapy given, whilst if it is low this can be kept well below 22 per cent. The nature of this factor is still not fully understood and research on the possible application of family therapy to reducing 'expressed emotion' is only just beginning.

As to the question of whether it is 'worth it', this is easier to answer. The important thing is that practitioners of family therapy can frequently observe important and significant changes occurring both in family organization and in the patient's problem after only a few sessions. In addition, this may happen without the 'side effects' of the patient becoming dependent on the therapist or of the family believing the solution to be out of their hands. The idea of bringing the whole family together, with fantasies of terrible family dramas erupting, may be daunting for some practitioners. The practitioner may believe that he could make a mistake and be responsible for 'breaking up the family'. This is highly unlikely.

Throughout this chapter I have been illustrating the powerful forces for stabilization occurring in all families, particularly in those families which are having difficulty in managing developmental transition.

● **8. Some Aspects of Family Therapy**

The goals of family therapists will vary widely but, almost universally, they are concerned to create an event in which some new **information** is put into the family. This information (Bateson 1973) is not some new data or knowledge that can be read in a book, but needs to be a different way of perceiving the events of which family members complain. This may occur through the family members being helped to understand the origins of the problem, through trying to understand or sharing unconscious fantasies, but it is more likely to take place through a series of interactions occurring in the session which relabel what had recently happened in a different way. In essence, the therapist attempts to create a family event which may be familiar in many ways, but he uses his knowledge of family organization to help the family resolve it or to end the sequence or 'dance' in a different way. By having a different experience, the family members may then experience differences that had previously been felt as unpleasant exchanges. For example, in one family in which there was a 16-year-old deaf daughter, and a 12-year-old boy who was not attending school and had been defined by the family as 'retarded', the mother complained that the whole load of worry about the family fell on her shoulders. Both she and her husband seemed to agree that the husband was 'distant, detached and disinterested'. The therapist suspected that this was a collusive relationship. That is, he believed the mother and the children (and the father as well) were all behaving in a way which kept the mother over-burdened and kept the father distant. The therapist believed that this view of the family was inefficient and was playing an important part in keeping the young boy behaving much less competently than he was able. In order to change this view of the roles of the mother and father, the therapist needed firstly to challenge the idea of the father being distant and secondly almost to stage-manage an event in which he and the mother begin to play their customary parts. An example of challenging the idea of the father being distant was initated by the therapist asking the father how his wife had coped when she realized her first child was deaf. The father answered that 'it took its toll'. The therapist pressed the father as to whom the mother had gained her support from; had it been from the children, had it been from her mother or had it been from him? The father answered, 'I don't know'.

From the way the family had been describing the father, the therapist could have predicted that the mother and father would 'agree' that this was because the father was disinterested. The therapist, however, defined the situation differently.

Therapist: 'It sounds like she does not tell you much about what she is thinking.'
Father: 'Probably not.'
Therapist: 'So you seem to get left out quite a lot.'
Father: 'No.'
Mother: 'No, he likes to be left out.'
The therapist now begins to challenge this definition.
Therapist to father: 'Just a minute. Is this really true?'
Father: 'I do, yes.'
Therapist: 'Ah, but who sold you the idea?'

The therapist continues to take this position until eventually the father responds by acknowledging that he actually finds it very difficult to play an active part in the family as he feels his wife has already decided everything. Which of these definitions of the father is 'true' is not that relevant. The importance is that the therapist has opened up an alternative way of viewing things. This couple were unaccustomed to continuing their disagreements to a point of resolution. Commonly, disagreements would end by the mother taking a decision, or by the children providing a diversion. In the presence of the therapist, both partners turned to him with their point of view, assuming that he would resolve the disagreement. It is at this point that the therapist deliberately provokes an event which ends in an unfamiliar way for the family. That is that the couple begin to face and resolve their differences.

Therapist: 'No! Sort it out together!' (To the wife) 'With him! *He*'s your husband not me!'
The mother finally turns to the father and complains.
Mother: 'I took Ben to the doctor's. I tried to get it all straightened out. You just spoke about it, but I did it.'
Father: 'Right.'
Therapist to father: 'Go on.'
Father: 'No, no, no.'

At this point, the therapist challenges the position the father is taking by defining him as compliant rather than as disinterested. The therapist asks the father, 'So is this what happens at home? She makes a speech and you say right?'. The therapist presses this issue until eventually the father confronts the mother with the fact that he feels unable to stand up to her as she is always much more verbal than he, so he eventually 'gives up and ignores her'. Subsequently, the couple begin to experiment with an alternative way of responding to each other, particularly in relation to their roles as parents. In doing this, the therapist has temporarily increased the level of conflict beyond the level which usually occurs in the family. The goal is not so much to help than to understand the conscious or unconscious 'reason' for their difficulties, but rather to experience a different view of their relationship so that they can begin to respond to the children and each other differently.

In general, family therapists would not see interpretation as a useful way of introducing this information. However, consider the following sequence:

A young girl of 11 is brought by her mother and step-father with the complaint that she is constantly crying. Her mother has complained that at times she has felt like strangling her and there was a time when she threatened to have her taken into care.

There were in the session two younger brothers who tended to observe in a rather distant way the interaction between Pamela and her mother. It is, however, significant that Pamela was nearing the age of 12, and it had not been acknowledged that the mother had had two previous families by different men. In both cases, the mother had left, or the family had broken up when the eldest reached the age of 12. In the third of the five sessions for which the family were seen, Pamela is fingering a little box, looking away and generally refusing to speak. The excerpt illustrates the interaction of the therapist, girl and family around the box, and the therapist's response.

Therapist: 'You keep showing that to me. It must be very important. What is it?'
Girl: 'It is a box.'
Therapist: 'Can I have a look? I feel I am supposed to see it. Am I allowed to look inside or don't you want to show it to me?'
Mother: 'I don't think there is anything in it, is there?'
Therapist: 'You decide, Pamela, is it private?'
Mother: 'It is all the silly things she brought out with her.'
Therapist: 'The family think it is all rubbish; is that right?'
Father: 'It is not rubbish, just her own things.'
Therapist: 'Yes, private things?'
Father: 'They are not really private, they are what girls of her age collect.'
    Girl pulls out broken bracelet and other broken trinkets from the box.
Therapist: 'I think it is very important that you carry all the different bits and pieces that are broken and keep them with you and look after them and that is rather like what my colleague thought Pamela is doing for the family; that she was doing some crying, that we didn't really understand what the crying was about yet, but carrying some of the broken things, things that have got broken in the past for the family and that that is why it was so unbearable for the family because she was carrying in her all these hurts and broken things which really you must have felt as well.'

In this example, a piece of behaviour is interpreted to represent an unconscious expression of a family dilemma. It is not suggested that this link is 'true' or 'untrue' but rather that it links in the girl's behaviour with that of the rest of the family.

● **9. Another Clinical Example**
The following case illustrates:
a. The tension between stability and change.
b. The intensity and repetitiveness of the sequences and patterns in the family; 'the family dance'.

c. The impact of change in the wider system (retirement and the stabilizing effect of the day hospital treatment).

d. The case therefore illustrates also the intervention of the family therapist in the wider system of family and professional.

Wendy was an only child, aged 20 when referred. Her mother, Anne, had not known her own mother and had been brought up by an aunt and her grandmother. She was nervous when she had Wendy and this was aggravated when the paediatrician suggested that Wendy may be partially sighted. This later turned out to be untrue, but it was one factor which pushed Wendy and her mother closer together in the first few years. Another factor was that the father Simon, aged 60, was often away. He had recently retired from an active life as an officer in the army. He had had long periods away from home on missions to which his family either could not, or had chosen not to follow him. Wendy and her mother continued to live in Scotland. Simon's retirement almost coincided with the time when Wendy would be leaving school and perhaps leaving home.

Eighteen months before referral to the family therapy clinic Wendy had been attending a day hospital run for the armed forces near her home in Scotland. She had been 'unable' to work because of 'obsessional rituals'. These involved washing and, most specifically, clothes washing rituals. She claimed that these were caused by 'contaminations', which she experienced in crowded places, particularly in two nearby towns where there happened to be many young soldiers, but also if accidentally touched by either of her parents. At home she was perceived by her parents, and behaved, as irritatingly incompetent. She would insist that her parents help her with any activity, writing a letter, filling the washing machine, etc. In the day hospital she attended groups with other patients, had the almost full attention of one senior nurse, spent two hours a week with her psychiatrist and was particularly attached to her psychologist. The latter had attempted several behavioural training programmes with frustrating results. The family was seen for some seventeen sessions during the course of 2½ years. These sessions began on a weekly basis. In the first session the therapist noted that as they came into the room the parents motioned Wendy where to sit, then they suggested which clothes she should remove for comfort and watched her anxiously if she was asked any questions, clearly ready with the 'correct' reply. Wendy, in the first session, found it almost impossible to say anything on her own behalf. She expected her parents to speak for her or that the therapist could rely on the report received from the other psychiatrists, nurses, psychologists, etc. The therapist chose to ignore the parents and repeatedly asked Wendy 'why had she come?'. Finally, and with great difficulty, she was able to say, 'It's because of the crossed wires.'.

In this first session it was clear that the family organization was one which supported Wendy remaining incompetent. This then brought the parents together in their relatively new role as shared parents (the father recently having retired). Wendy was now behaving in a way which was appropriate to a much younger child. The therapist began to challenge the parents' interruptions, observed the way in which Wendy would 'activate' them to speak and blocked this behaviour. Gradually, Wendy began to take on more responsibilities at home, but despite this continued to attend the day hospital. The therapist realized that the latter was providing Wendy with a life which was richer than anything she could conceive of outside. Having no siblings and no friends, she had little impetus for change. The therapist asked her whether her parents would welcome the effect on her which more independence would bring (such as speaking up for herself more clearly, taking a more independent line, etc.). To the great surprise and shock of her parents she answered, 'No, I don't think they are ready, I think they would prefer me to remain a baby.'. The therapist suggested that perhaps the day hospital was a good solution for everyone. It allowed the parents to continue to feel they were doing the 'right thing' by their daughter and it allowed Wendy to have a life, apparently as an adult, while in reality she was treated as a child. The therapist suggested that maybe this is what they should settle for and prescribed caution about any abrupt change. He left the family without offering another appointment. Two weeks later the therapist received a letter from Wendy, the first that she had written herself, saying that she had discharged herself from the day hospital and would like another consultation for the family. The therapist had realized that two aspects of the wider system were playing an important part in Wendy's problems; the father's retirement from an institution on which he was highly dependent (the army), and Wendy's involvement in an institution on which she was highly dependent (the day hospital), the staff of which the therapist believed responded with anxiety whenever she made a bid for more independence. It was relatively useless to challenge the repetitive family sequences without also addressing the stabilizing effects of the wider system. Thus, by suggesting the family settle for the status quo with Wendy remaining a patient in the day hospital, the therapist had forced both Wendy and her parents to face their conflict about change and to make a real choice. From this point on, therapy moved more quickly but, after discharge from the day hospital, Wendy complained more acutely of her 'contaminations'. The therapist suggested that the family should not attempt to 'cure' these, but rather they should think of them as a problem of loneliness. That is, that 'nobody could understand just exactly what Wendy felt like when having these feelings'. He therefore asked Wendy if she would agree to her parents making these feelings worse so that she could describe them with more passion and the parents could understand them more fully. He therefore asked the parents to push Wendy into crowded places and touch her whenever possible, for one week. The parents were amazed when Wendy agreed to this, as they had always avoided confrontation with her and accommodated her every request. The mother then acknowledged that she had a phobia about cats and the father and Wendy agreed to bring cats into the house to do the same thing for her. Finally, the father acknowledged that he had a phobia of heights and the mother and Wendy agreed to take the father for a walk along the nearby cliffs. This session ended with great jocularity and on their return, not surprisingly, they had been unable to elicit the expected symptoms in any of these situations. Thus, the symptoms had ceased to have a stabilizing influence in the family and had become part of a more playful behaviour which allowed more freedom and experimentation.

Later aspects of the therapy were concerned with helping Wendy to think how to get a job without her parents doing it for her, helping the mother to take charge of the father, so that he became less anxious and therefore less intrusive on Wendy and, finally, helping Wendy independently to leave home and find her own lodgings. Only then was she able to make friends and develop her own life.

In this case, the initial interventions were of a type described as direct intervention in the process of the session. However, the intervention which prescribed that Wendy should remain in the day hospital as a fitting solution to her and her parents' requirements of each other was designed to give to the family a caricature of an aspect of their shared perceptions of each other which was not acknowledged. This rather exaggerated portrayal created a crisis which allowed Wendy to leave the hospital and she and her parents to begin to be more courageous in facing issues of change.

• **10. Different Methods of Therapy with the Family**
The kind of direct approach described in the second example does rely on the family members making an alliance for family change with the therapist. This, in turn, requires that the pressures for stability are not so great that the opportunities for change cannot be welcomed. When the family is thoroughly entrenched in a particular pattern, the members may be at a loss to experiment with alternatives or may see any alternative as a great threat.

In these situations, it is common for the therapist to adopt a more 'strategic' approach which often uses tasks which are not obviously directed toward change or may even be apparently prescribing what is already happening (Haley 1977). The most coherent body of such work has been developed by the Centre for Family Studies in Milan (Pallazzoli et al. 1978). There is not, however, space in this chapter for further elaboration of this approach. Other approaches particularly explore the intergenerational patterns running through the family and may involve grandparents and extended family members in exploring these. The goal of this is to help the family members to feel less 'programmed' and more able to take autonomous decisions.

What is common in all the approaches, however, is that in general the therapist is less concerned with pathology and with dysfunction, and more concerned with blocking dysfunction and encouraging the discovery of latent or new repertoires of behaviour in the family.

• **11. Family Therapy, Group Psychotherapy, and Individual Therapy**
The last sections gave a taste of the operation of family therapy. Particularly in the first example, the therapist attempted to achieve small changes in sequence or pattern in the session as they occurred. Naturally, such small changes are not lasting, unless they are repeated with sufficient intensity and frequency that they become part of a new folklore in the family. Only at this point can such changes be generalized from the specific issues under discussion to other aspects of family life, so that there can be a real shift in the organization of the family. This is quite different from the approach of other psychotherapies, detailed elsewhere in this volume. At this point it may be useful to clarify some of the differences between what I have called family of 'natural' group therapy, in comparison with 'stranger' group therapy (i.e. when the group is formed from strangers for the purpose of therapy) and with individual psychotherapy. These are summarized in the following chart (*Fig.* 1).

INDIVIDUAL THERAPY	STRANGER GROUP THERAPY	NATURAL (FAMILY) GROUP THERAPY
1. The patient/therapist relationship exists only as a context for therapy	1. The group exists only as a context for therapy	1. The family has a life of its own, with a history and an anticipated future
2. Therapy occurs in the context of the intensity of relationship between therapist and patient	2. Therapy occurs in the context of the intensity of relationships between the therapist and group members, and between group members	2. Therapy occurs in context of a change in relationship pattern in the context of the current intense family relationships
3. Thus — the therapist is central	3. Thus — at different times the therapist or some part of the group may be central	3. Thus — the therapist is principally an agent of change rather than a central actor
4. The therapist *allows* the intensity of affect from the patient to him/her to develop (although the setting may provoke it)	4. The therapist facilitates the 'integration' or 'gelling' of the group in the service of therapy	4. The therapist is more likely to be concerned to develop the differentiation of the group
5. Therapist and patient maintain a non-social relationship (to varying degrees depending on the model)	5. The members are discouraged from meeting between sessions	5. The members remain in an intense relationship between sessions
6. The therapist does not try to develop structure in the therapeutic relationship, and interpretations may be used to highlight inappropriate structural patterns sought by the patient. In child psychotherapy the therapist *may* be forced to be a parental adult	6. There is no permanent structural organization of the group. That which evolves is transient and often seen by the therapist as a recreation of past or 'inner' families of the members. The members are usually of similar age, as may be the therapist. The therapist aims to be 'meta' to the group	6. The family has an inherent and necessary hierarchical organization, relating to the different ages, developmental positions and responsibilities of the members. As the therapist is an adult, this will affect how he/she is used by the family. The therapist aims to *think* from a meta-position, but may *act* in a partisan manner
7. Change occurs through understanding the meaning of an old pattern in a new context. This change has then to be generalized to other contexts. The pattern in the original context may or *may not* change	7. Change occurs through understanding the meaning of an old pattern in a new context. This change has then to be generalized to other contexts. The pattern in the original context may or *may not* change	7. Change occurs through changing the pattern in an 'old' context, so that the context itself is changed

●   **12. Applications to Different Kinds of Family Structure and 'Non-family' Human Systems**

An obvious question is: for what diagnostic categories is family therapy applicable? The goal of family therapy is not to remove a 'cause', but rather to interfere with patterns which maintain a problem and to promote the development of more healthy patterns. This can be applied in any context where such an agreement can be worked out, and yet it has been found to be a particularly potent form of therapy in the behavioural and psychosomatic disorders of children, in neurotic and relationship problems in adults and in substance abuse. In addition, it has been used with the families of schizophrenics, particularly those in the process of rehabilitation, and in families where there is a seriously ill or dying member, or the consequences of a recent bereavement.

The model of family on which the illustrations have been based, for convenience rather than for truth, has been that of the traditional nuclear family. Many people, however, do not live in the tidy group of 2 parents and 2.4 children. Three family structures are of particular importance:

a. Single parent families, whether as a result of divorce, bereavement or the lack of a partner.

b. Extended family organizations as, for example, when a young couple or a single parent live with their parents and perhaps siblings.

c. Remarried families, sometimes called blended families or reconstituted families.

For each of these three structures there are particular issues of which the therapist needs to be aware and incorporate in his views concerning intervention. In the single parent family, the parent needs more support and non family social contacts take on greater significance. However, the parent's authority may have to be more autocratic, or he/she may need to delegate authority to the elder siblings. One can easily see what can go wrong when an elder sibling takes authority unilaterally. Alternatively, if a parent responds to the loneliness of being single by befriending the children, he or she may then be unable to help them make the necessary developmental transitions.

In the extended family organization, there is a particular danger of confusion between the roles of parents and grandparents. For example, will the grandparents' support be seen as underpinning or undermining the parents' authority, and how can the parent help the grandparent find a useful role which is not in competition with him or her? In addition, the children and the grandparent may be allied against the parent. In a positive way, this may allow the child freedom of access to someone with whom they are less emotionally involved, but in a negative way it may be perceived by the parent as 'stealing their child'.

In the remarried family, all these issues are still poignant, but in addition:

i. The problem of the children resolving the conflict of loyalty between the step-parent and the absent parent continues to be an issue and it depends particularly on the degree to which, for example, the divorced couple are still fighting or have accepted the new liaison.

ii. There is also the problem of the children having changed their 'position' in the family. Thus, an elder child in the original family may have half brothers or sisters who are older, and find him or herself becoming the younger child or vice versa.

Each different structure has its own strengths and weaknesses in terms of the goal of promoting the development of the children. The job for the family therapist is firstly to understand the organization and structure in which the people live, and secondly to plan his or her interventions on the basis of what is most functional for that family at that time. For example, in the single parent family it may be appropriate to encourage the mother to rely more on an elder sibling for certain functions such as helping with the younger children. In another family, this may have happened to a degree where the elder sibling is in competition with her. In the latter case, she may need to be helped to re-establish her authority so that an appropriate generational boundary develops between her and the elder child.

Thus, the task for the therapist is to think about the organization and functioning of the system and to use him or herself to create a new balance in the dilemma between stability and change. This thinking can then be applied to a child living in a children's home, to a school classroom situation or, with certain modifications, to a social delivery agency or even an industrial organization.

• 13. What can the Practitioner do?

The training of nearly all practitioners, whether in medicine, psychology or social work, has underlined the individual integrity of the patient. This chapter has been about seeing the patient as part of a wider system, the family and 'others', and seeing his or her problems as in part a manifestation of those relationships.

I would like to feel that this chapter has introduced the practitioner to the process of thinking in terms of relationships, rather than cause, and to consider the whole system rather than just its parts. I hope it has also illustrated how the family therapist can use this thinking to engage actively in the processes of the family. Of course, he or she is then also *part* of the system which is struggling between stability and change. To a degree, all therapists and practitioners are part of the system which they treat. This was well illustrated in the case of Wendy and her therapist in the day hospital. I hope that the practitioner will be stimulated to think how to increase the competence in the family rather than the incompetence. *As well as thinking of the consequences* of giving a remedy such as tranquillizers, the practitioner might anticipate the effects for the whole system of *not* giving a remedy. Lastly, I hope I have demonstrated that the practitioner may need to develop and maintain a quite different perspective from that held by the family members, and to think how to engender a different set of perceptions in those who are concerned to achieve a change. I have also described in some detail some of the forces in a family which tend towards the maintenance of stability. It is, therefore, not surprising that when a practitioner offers what he or she thinks are rational solutions, they are frequently not welcomed as warmly as might be hoped. In fact, to get through this, the practitioner may often need to think of solutions which are quite 'irrational' in every day terms. One such was used in the case of Wendy.

However, this chapter has not provided a recipe on how to 'do family therapy'. Learning from the written word has severe limitations in acquiring any active skill. In the final section some useful reading is listed, as well as more useful suggestions as to how the practitioner can acquire skill in understanding and intervening in families.

• 14. Further Reading and Opportunities for Learning and Training

For those who want to read further I would suggest the simplest book is *Working with Families* by Gill Gorell Barnes (1984). There is also a selection of papers published in the *Journal of The Royal Society of Medicine* (1985) on Family Work in General Practice. Perhaps the clearest exposition is in three books by Salvador Minuchin; the first is *Families and Family Therapy* (1974); the second is *Psychosomatic Families* op. cit.; and the most recent is *Family Therapy Techniques* (1981). For a clearer exposition of a slightly different, but related, approach, I would recommend reading *Problem Solving Therapy* by Jay Haley (op. cit).

However, the best way for the practitioner to develop some skills is to join up with one or more colleagues, who have decided to explore their thinking and work with families. They can use discussion, observe each other's work, perhaps play tape recordings, or arrange sessions together and consult each other. The forming of such a group can allow the development of the inventiveness and imagination of the members, essential ingredients for working with families. Details of how to carry out this kind of consultation/supervision are also the subject of many of the courses which are provided by the institutions listed below. Information on conferences, a journal and local courses are available from the Association for Family Therapy, 6 Heol Seddon, Danes Court, Llandaff, Cardiff, CF5 2QX. In recent years, the British Postgraduate Medical Federation has run courses for general practitioners, and there are courses run at independent institutes in London (The Institute of Family Therapy, 43 New Cavendish Street, London, W.1. Tel: 01–935 1651), and Cardiff (The Family Institute, 15 Cathedral Road, Cardiff. Tel: 0222–28747).

There are also courses run at Newcastle Polytechnic and at the University of Birmingham, in Bristol, North Wales and Manchester as well as Scotland and Ireland. Lists of organizations providing these and other courses are available from the Association for Family Therapy.

• References

Ashby W. R. (1956) *Introduction to cybernetics*. John Wiley New York and London.
Bateson G. (1973) *Steps towards an ecology of mind*. Paladin, St. Albans.
Bertalanffy L. V. (1968) *General System Theory*. Brazillier, New York.
Cooklin A. I. (1973) Consideration of the 'contract' between staff and patient and its relationship to current hospital practice. *Br. J. Med. Psychol.* **45**, 279–285.
Gorell Barnes G. (1984) *Working with families*. Macmillan/BASW, London.
Gurman A. S. and Kniskern D. P. (1981) *Handbook of Family Therapy*. Brunner/Mazel, New York.

Haley J. (1977) *Problem Solving Therapy*. Jossey-Bass, California.

Jackson D. D. (1957) The question of family homeostasis. *Psychiatry Quarterly Supplement* **31**, 79–80.

Leff J., Kuipers L., Berkowitz R. et al. (1982) A controlled trial of social intervention in the families of schizophrenic patients. *Br. J. Psychiatry* **141**, 121–134.

Minuchin S. (1974) *Families and Family Therapy*. Tavistock Publications, London.

Minuchin S., Rosman B. and Baker L. (1978) *Psychosomatic families*. Harvard University Press, Cambridge, Mass.

Minuchin S. and Fishman C. (1981) *Family Therapy Techniques*. Harvard University Press, Cambridge, Mass.

Mossige S., Petterson R. B. and Blaker R. M. (1979) Egocentrism and inefficiency in the communication of families containing a schizophrenic member. *Family Process* **18**, 405–425.

Pallazzoli M. S., Boscolo L., Cecchin G. et al. (1978) *Paradox and counter paradox: A new model in the therapy of the family in schizophrenic transaction*. Jason Aronson, London and New York.

Royal Society of Medicine (1985) Selected papers on family work in general practice. *J. Roy. Soc. Med.* No. 8, Vol. 78.

8

Behaviour therapy

by Alan King

Although behaviour therapy is a relatively straightforward form of psychological treatment an adequate definition of it is, necessarily, rather lengthy. Unlike most other forms of psychotherapy it cannot be entirely defined on the basis of theory. Its effects, and various phenomena which have been observed during research into behaviour therapy, have been partially explained in terms of learning theory which derives from the work of Pavlov and of Skinner into classical and operant conditioning. Learning theory has not, however, proved to be a perfect model. In fact, the techniques which so characterize behaviour therapy are used not because their effect has been predicted according to theory, but because experience has demonstrated it. Furthermore, many of the techniques of modern behaviour therapy can be traced back to methods of treatment described in medical writings which long predate the evolution of learning theory. Behaviour therapy, therefore, is essentially *empirical* rather than theoretical and is best defined in descriptive terms.

Just as characteristic as its techniques, with their emphasis upon overt behaviour, is the particular approach which behaviour therapy takes towards clinical problems. In contrast to other forms of psychotherapy, which seek to examine the historical antecedents of a problem, behaviour therapy is *symptom orientated*. As far as the behaviourist is concerned symptoms include not only the subjective experiences which tell us we are unwell, but inappropriate behaviours, disturbing thoughts and abnormal emotional states. Behaviour therapy is directed towards the relief of these symptoms and this has made it relatively easy to establish specific therapeutic goals, a feature which gives behaviour therapy some of its structure. This is reinforced by the use of written or verbal contracts and by the application of specified *time-limits* which are negotiated before treatment begins. Time-limiting a treatment programme is possible because behavioural treatments tend to be *short-term* so that the likely duration of therapy can be predicted. The precise duration of treatment is variable, depending upon the condition which is being treated, but six to ten sessions represent an average therapeutic investment. The therapist's style is outstandingly *directive* rather than reflective or interpretive and he, as well as the subject takes an *active* role in treatment, with *collaboration* between them being an intrinsic feature of the process.

Behaviour therapy has been applied with varying degrees of success in a wide range of disorders and new applications continue to be discovered. As far as its *clinical uses* are concerned, there is a spectrum of therapeutic styles which reflects differences in the various problems it is used to treat, and in the clientèle which presents them. On one hand, the subject who has a neurotic disorder tends to be well motivated for change through treatment. He is usually his own advocate and, as well as a behavioural component, his complaint includes physical and emotional symptoms which are causing him distress. By contrast, the subject in an institution for the chronically mentally disordered is generally poorly motivated for change. Usually, the complaint is made by a member of staff and is confined specifically to the subject's behaviour. These differences require rather distinct therapeutic approaches.

In the management of neurosis, negotiation and explanation are fundamental features. Therapy is client-directed, the subject is responsible for seeing through his own programme and the observations by which progress is judged are based mainly upon his own subjective experience and personal records. However, though the results which can be achieved using operant methods in the management of the chronically mentally disordered do appear to improve if effective negotiation and explanation are possible, these features are rather less important here than they are in the treatment of neurosis. At the same time, the subject's conscious co-operation and collaboration tend to be equally less crucial. Finally, operant programmes are under the control of staff who also carry out the observations and data recording by which treatment progress is measured.

● Behaviour Therapy in the Neuroses

Assessment

Identification of the problem is the first task. Depending upon whose opinion is asked, there may be several views about what constitutes the problem. Initially, at least, the subject's own view, defined as clearly and as free from jargon as possible, is the one which is adopted. Alternatives are recorded and introduced later if necessary. A full psychiatric assessment will identify important aspects such as current life stresses and any co-existing physical or psychiatric disorder which may influence a behavioural treatment. Details of past and present treatment may suggest interventions which are likely to prove effective and the assessment is not complete without some inquiry into the use of alcohol and tranquillizers, both of which can interfere with some forms of behavioural treatment.

The rest of the assessment, called a *functional* or *behavioural* analysis, is characteristic of the behavioural approach. This consists of a highly detailed account of the current determinants of the problem rather than of its historical antecedents. Predisposing factors, like heredity or early formative experiences, indicate why the subject should develop this particular problem and not another. Precipitating factors, like major life events, tell us why the problem should develop when it did. Behaviour therapy, however, is interested in a third group, the perpetuating factors. These are the 'here and now' reasons why the problem has continued long after the precipitating factors have ceased to exert their effect. If the perpetuating factors can be overcome then the problem ought to improve.

The analysis is made easier by examining the perpetuating factors under three headings (see *Fig.* 2):

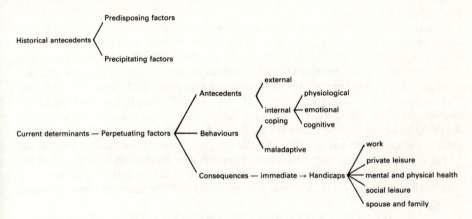

Fig. 2. The functional analysis of the problem.

1. *The antecedents ('As')*, or cues, may be external or internal. External cues include objects, situations, animals or people which immediately evoke the subject's symptoms. If these symptoms can be reproduced during the assessment session, either by introducing a relevant cue or by instructing the subject to carry out a simple manoeuvre such as overbreathing, immediate access is gained to the second group of cues. Internal cues are (*a*) physical, such as the bodily experiences which result from the physiological accompaniments of anxiety, (*b*) emotional, such as the fear experienced by phobic subjects and (*c*) cognitive, such as the disturbing thoughts and images which are so much a part of neurotic disorders.

2. *The behaviours ('Bs')* are the subject's overt responses. Those which maintain and strengthen the problem also restrict the subject's life in some way. They include avoidance, escape behaviours and ritualistic behaviours such as checking, cleaning and repeating. Sometimes the subject has discovered ways of coping with his problem such that the restrictions to his life are minimized. One of the tasks of treatment may be to improve upon these at the same time as overcoming the maladaptive behaviours by which the subject's life is handicapped.

3. *The consequences ('Cs')*. Although the subject's response to his discomfort has the effect of relieving it, this occurs at the *price* of ever-increasing restrictions to his life. In addition, maladaptive behaviours are reinforced by the very fact that they relieve discomfort immediately. The problem may be made worse by the efforts of family and friends who, in their desire to be of help and to deal with the problem, inadvertently reinforce it.

Eventually, as the disorder develops, immediate restrictions become major handicaps which are commonly the reasons why professional help is sought. Important areas of life which are affected include work, personal leisure, domestic functioning and interpersonal relationships. As well as causing handicaps in just those areas which will later provide an arena for the subject to tackle his problem, neurotic disorders cause secondary handicaps in other areas of life which may not be directly related to the initial problem.

Preparing for treatment

By ensuring that the subject fully understands the principles and implications of behaviour therapy and that he knows what is likely to be expected of him in treatment, the therapist is able to maximize the chances that treatment will be accepted and minimize the risk of subsequent drop-out. A Socratic method of explanation compliments the common-sense approach of behaviour therapy. The rationale of treatment is explained and any odd ideas the subject may have about behaviour therapy are examined so that they do not discourage him from agreeing to a programme which is otherwise acceptable. Any distressing physical symptoms are discussed in full and their psychophysiological basis is explained. This not only indicates that the therapist appreciates the subject's distress, but the more understanding the subject has of the nature of his symptoms, the less they will bother him and the less he will be troubled by fears of their possible consequences.

An explanation about treatment should cover several specific points:

1. Treatment is *client-directed*. Nothing is done without prior negotiation, no surprises are sprung upon the unsuspecting subject and his agreement is sought before any potentially distressing procedure is introduced. The therapist should always be prepared to take the same risks as those he expects of his client.

2. Most progress will be made *between* treatment sessions, during which time the subject is expected to complete, regularly and frequently, agreed 'homework' tasks. These may be time-consuming, so the subject's application is essential and other activities may have to be relegated in importance at least until treatment is completed.

3. It is likely, though not essential for treatment to be effective, that programmes involving exposure to feared situations will evoke discomfort. However, this discomfort will decline, or habituate, if exposure is sufficiently prolonged. For the subject's benefit habituation can be demonstrated either by devising an anxiety-provoking situation during the interview or by pointing out the way in which the subject's interview-related anxiety has declined since the start of the session.

4. Tasks are tackled in a gradual fashion so that initial success with easier tasks restores confidence for more difficult ones. A formal hierarchy may be used but is not essential. Tasks should be repeatable and, as well as being components of treatment, it is ideal if they involve an additional pay-off for the subject.

5. Treatment is usually time-limited. Progress is reassessed after an agreed number of sessions to decide whether further contact is likely to be worthwhile.

6. A friend or relative may be recruited and 'trained' to act as a cotherapist because it is unlikely that the therapist will be able to afford sufficient time to supervise all sessions.

7. Before treatment begins, specific *therapeutic targets* are established for each problem. Targets should be:
— precisely described in behavioural terms
— realistic
— relevant to the problem and representative of progress
— morally and legally acceptable

—desirable for the subject

Recreating the subject's problem and symptoms during the assessment session is a great help towards deciding whether behavioural methods will be both suitable and acceptable. The height phobic, for example, may be asked to climb as far as he can up a fire-escape. This simple manoeuvre, called a *behavioural test*, not only leaves the subject in no doubt as to what may be expected of him in treatment but it provides an unambiguous behavioural measure of the severity of his problem and indicates the level at which treatment must begin. It is also a convenient moment to test whether behavioural methods are likely to prove effective. The therapist uses prompting, praise and modelling to persuade the subject to improve upon his performance. The longer the subject tolerates the situation, the more likely his symptoms are to habituate and the more progress he will make. His performance here is a good indicator of how co-operative he will be in treatment and the therapist is given an opportunity to identify and discuss the subject's current coping strategies and any irrational ideas which might be maintaining his symptoms unnecessarily. It is, of course, a first step in treatment and, if it is carried out properly, *a test of behaviour therapy* leaves the subject with a sense of achievement from the first contact.

Measurement and record keeping

Behaviour therapists like their subjects to measure items like symptom severity, problem severity and the degree of handicap in key areas of life. Measures applied before and after treatment and at follow-up indicate treatment progress, overall effectiveness and the durability of treatment. The ease of measurement has not only made efficacy studies possible, but it has important clinical implications, because the subject discovers that limits can now be applied to a symptom or problem which previously seemed to be boundless.

Standard questionnaires are available for some items but for a symptom such as anxiety a simple, visual analogue scale is quite sufficient. Its range is a matter of personal preference. Some therapists like to use a 0 to 8 scale and others prefer 0 to 100. In either case, 0 represents the total absence of the symptom and the top of the scale represents the most severe the symptom has ever been. Somewhere between the two is a level at which the symptom becomes tolerable. It may be useful to incorporate this level into treatment targets. With a little instruction on the use of these scales, most subjects achieve a level of reliability from which treatment progress can be assessed.

Behaviour therapists also like their subjects to keep records in the form of a *daily diary*. This would contain information about task completion and associated symptom severity. A diary is also useful for getting at the cognitive components of a problem, because relevant details can be recorded as they occur. As well as providing information for the subject and therapist to process at their next meeting, the need to produce a diary encourages work on task assignments. The effort which has gone into producing a diary is also a good indicator of motivation in cases of doubt.

Factors influencing suitability for treatment

In the individual case, suitability for treatment depends upon certain features of the problem and upon factors in the client. The problem should be:
  1. Current.

2. Predictable.
3. Repetitive.
4. Describable in behavioural terms.
5. Measurable.
6. Sufficiently disabling to warrant the necessary therapeutic investment.
    The client should:
1. Understand and accept treatment.
2. Not exhibit any psychiatric disorder which would contraindicate the use of behaviour therapy. No contraindications are absolute but four are important:
   — severe depression
   — some forms of organic brain damage
   — active psychosis
   — a disorder of personality which results in the subject's inability to stick to a structured treatment programme

The diagnosis alone is a reliable guide as to whether or not a problem is likely to be suitable for behaviour therapy. For some conditions, behaviour therapy is the treatment of choice. These are:
   — simple phobias
   — social anxiety and social skills dysfunction
   — agoraphobia
   — obsessive–compulsive rituals
   — psychosexual dysfunction
   — some childhood disorders such as school refusal

There are many other conditions in which behaviour therapy has a role, though not necessarily as the treatment of choice. This list is not exhaustive:
   — depression
   — alcoholism
   — drug abuse
   — smoking
   — appetitive disorders
   — habit disorders and tics
   — hypochondriasis
   — obsessional thoughts and ruminations
   — grief reactions
   — anxiety states
   — marital dysfunction
   — child abuse
   — compulsive gambling
   — some childhood disorders

Working out a treatment package

The range of techniques which is available usually means that more than one approach can be offered to treat any given problem. In many cases, a package consisting of various techniques is used. The therapist may present the full range of techniques to the subject, cafeteria-style, with advice about the implications of each. The subject may be given the choice of those which he thinks will suit him best, though it must be said that the therapist does guide the choice and would strongly advise a technique if it was particularly indicated for a specific problem.

As treatment progresses, the focus of therapy may switch from one problem to another. This is not unreasonable and behaviour therapy is flexible enough to accommodate such changes. However, the experienced therapist is always alert to the subject whose attention shifts from problem to problem so frequently that it is impossible to do much effective work upon any of them.

Efficacy, limitations and therapeutic failures

The disorders in which behaviour therapy may be usefully employed account for one in eight of psychiatric out-patient referrals. The effectiveness of behaviour therapy has been demonstrated in a number of controlled trials and single-case studies. For example, because behaviour therapy is orientated towards the relief of symptoms, it has been suggested that its failure to deal with any underlying neurotic conflict might result in the emergence of fresh symptoms, a phenomenon known as *symptom substitution*. In fact, what evidence there is suggests that this occurs rarely, if at all. Furthermore, treatment gains appear not only to be maintained in the long run, but there is a progressive improvement in various areas of life following behaviour therapy.

Behavioural programmes are, however, not always successful. There are several reasons for this, some of which are avoidable. The commonest, perhaps, is a subject's failure to comply with the agreed treatment programme. This may be because treatment tasks are too difficult or because co-existing life stresses are interfering with therapy. Some subjects are discouraged by counter-instructions from friends, neighbours or family. Obsessional subjects may use mental 'tricks' (*internal avoidance*) to 'make good' the omission of a ritual. Where exposure methods are used, too short an exposure session is not only ineffective but may even make the problem worse and there is a very small group of subjects whose anxiety fails to habituate even with prolonged exposure. Occasionally, the problem has been misidentified, with the result that treatment targets are wrong. Finally, there may be a co-existing psychiatric disorder such as depression. Severe depression interferes with between-session improvements, even when there is good progress within treatment sessions. It must be treated before lasting therapeutic gains can be made.

• Behaviour therapy in institutions

The skills which are required for independent living are frequently deficient in the behavioural repertoire of subjects who are cared for in the institutions for the chronically mentally disordered. In mental handicap these skills may never have been acquired and in chronic mental illness, particularly in chronic schizophrenia, skills may have been lost due to the ravages of the primary disorder or as a result of prolonged institutionalization. In some cases, aggressive, destructive and bizarre behaviours have taken their place. The aims of treatment are:
1. To improve the quality of life of the subject.
2. To establish the skills necessary for life in the community.
3. To eliminate unwanted behaviours which constitute major management problems

The methods used are based upon the principles of *operant conditioning* which predict that behaviours are influenced by their consequences. Whenever possible, operant programmes emphasize the reinforcement of desirable behaviours. Aversive methods are used only when positive reinforcement and other methods of treatment have failed. The subject, his relatives and the staff must be fully informed of the aims and methods of treatment and the rights, privileges and standards of care of subjects should be rigorously maintained.

According to the principles of operant conditioning, the reinforcer should be delivered as soon as possible following the behaviour it is intended to reinforce. This is relatively simple where the therapist is working on a one-to-one basis with an individual. However, where few staff supervise many subjects the practical problems of selecting and delivering the requisite reinforcer for each individual is overcome by the use of tokens (*secondary reinforcers*) which are contingent upon the required behaviour. Tokens may be exchanged later for goods and privileges (*primary reinforcers*).

Such programmes, known as *token economies*, have been criticized on academic and ethical grounds and the role of tokens as conditioned reinforcers has been questioned. Nevertheless, token economies do seem to be useful for producing desirable behavioural changes in subjects and, perhaps, in the staff who supervise them.

• Commonly Used Behavioural Techniques

Methods of increasing desirable behaviours

An event which increases the likelihood that a behaviour will recur is a reinforcer. *Positive reinforcement* involves the addition of something that is equivalent to a reward and *negative reinforcement* involves the removal of something that is aversive. Each increases the likelihood of recurrence of any behaviour upon which it is contingent. Sweets are useful as reinforcers for children, and tobacoo, money and privileges for adults. The nature of the reinforcer depends upon the likes and dislikes of the individual and in all cases it is gradually replaced by social reinforcement as targets are achieved.

In *shaping*, behaviours are achieved by reinforcing small steps or approximations towards the final response. *Chaining* involves the sequential linking of the component responses which constitute an organized behaviour with reinforcement being contingent only upon the final response in the chain. Chaining is often most easily carried out in reverse, beginning with the terminal response and progressively building up prior behaviours. Responses can be initiated by verbal or physical *prompting* or by *modelling* in which the therapist demonstrates the required behaviour to the subject. *Fading* involves gradually withdrawing prompts, as the behaviour is achieved.

These simple procedures have been applied with success to a range of human behaviours. Although operant methods are usually associated with the management of problems in institutions, it will be clear that the principles of reinforcement are equally fundamental to the treatment of neurotic disorders.

Indeed in some, such as certain forms of marital therapy, an operant approach may be the central feature of treatment.

Methods of reducing undesirable behaviours

Aversive techniques, which employ noxious stimuli to eliminate unwanted behaviours, were once used extensively in the management of sexual deviations, alcoholism, drug abuse and certain specific behaviours like self-mutilation, which are seen in institutions. Electric shocks and chemically-induced nausea were commonly used as aversive stimuli but the methods lost popularity partly because results were rather disappointing. In some instances, particularly with the mentally handicapped, aversive stimuli can paradoxically reinforce the undesirable behaviour.

Removing the subject from all reinforcers, called 'time out', is a form of *extinction* procedure in which unwanted behaviours gradually disappear because they are no longer reinforced. The use of aversive stimuli in imagination is called *covert sensitization* and has been used particularly in the management of deviant sexual behaviours and urges. It involves the client imagining himself performing the deviant act and this is interrupted by an aversive scene, such as the approach of a policeman to arrest him for his behaviour.

The therapeutic component of the behavioural management of obsessive-compulsive rituals is called *response prevention*. It consists of preventing the subject from indulging in a ritual until the urge to do so has passed. Teaching a subject to interrupt intrusive, obsessional thoughts by shouting 'stop' is called *thought stopping*. The subject then learns to internalize the order so that he can use the technique in any situation. Tics and habit disorders are managed by instructing the subject to follow the unwanted behaviour with one which is incompatible with it, a method known as *habit reversal*. Alternatively, the subject may be instructed to practise the unwanted behaviour until he tires of it. This is *satiation* or *massed practice*.

Self-observation, a feature of all *self-control* methods, can reduce the frequency of unwanted behaviours, like cigarette smoking, by itself. It may be combined with *self-reinforcement*, where the subject rewards himself for periods of desirable behaviour, or *self-punishment* for failure to achieve an agreed target. A financial penalty is called a *response cost*. Reducing the opportunity for a behaviour by manipulating the conditions under which it occurs is known as *stimulus control* and has been used to treat appetitive disorders and alcohol abuse.

Methods of reducing anxiety and fear

Exposure to feared situations can be carried out slowly or rapidly. *Slow exposure, desensitization*, involves inducing a state of relaxation before a feared stimulus is introduced. Anxiety is minimized by choosing stimuli from a hierarchy of cues of increasing difficulty, hence the term *systematic desensitization*, and by interrupting exposure as soon as the subject indicates arousal. The stimulus is reintroduced only when a state of relaxation has been re-established. It is supposed to work by weakening the fear-evoking property of the stimulus by presenting it only during relaxation — a state which is incompatible with fear. This principle is known as reciprocal inhibition. It is a slow, tedious method which has been largely superceded by *rapid exposure*. Here, anxiety is permitted but exposure is prolonged so that *habituation* occurs. When carried out *in vivo* it is sometimes called *flooding* and its use in imagination, at which time maximal anxiety levels are evoked, is called *implosion*. Exposure is useful whenever there is avoidance of feared situations. Its effect is impaired by depression and by excessive use of alcohol and tranquillizers.

Relaxation therapy can take several forms though none seems to be more effective than another. Methods commonly involve progressive muscular relaxation or mental imagery. Taped instructions are useful and it is usual to link the relaxed state with a pleasant, imagined scene so that relaxation can be induced in any situation merely by recalling the scene.

Biofeedback consists of providing the subject with information about the state of his physiological functioning. One of the physiological accompaniments of anxiety, such as heart rate, galvanic skin response (GSR) or electro-myogram (EMG) is converted, electronically, into a visual or auditory signal. The subject learns to alter the signal and so his state of arousal. It has been used to treat generalized tension and anxiety. Migraine, tension headaches and other muscular dysfunctions may also respond.

Methods of altering social behaviours

Difficulties in forming and sustaining relationships with others are commonly associated with psychiatric disorders. *Social skills training* aims to modify a subject's social behaviour in order to help him to overcome these difficulties. There is some evidence that social skills training produces an improvement in overall psychological adjustment as well as in social competence.

Treatment usually involves a programmed course which is applied to a group of selected subjects. Behaviours are modelled by the therapist and the group follows this with role-play and rehearsal under controlled conditions. The therapist's role is to guide, coach and encourage the group. Group members offer feedback with an initial emphasis upon successful aspects of performance. Shortcomings are examined later. Closed-circuit television and video play-back can be invaluable during feedback. Social interactions are examined in terms of separate components such as eye contact, posture, speaking skills, etc. This makes the role-play more manageable for the group and it helps to structure feedback. Exercises increase in complexity as skills develop.

Cognitive methods

For centuries it has been recognized that the influence of events upon our psychological equilibrium owes more to our attitudes towards those events than to their exact nature. In behaviour therapy a cognition is usually taken to be a thought. Those which are important in generating and maintaining dysphoric symptoms occur automatically and so rapidly, that they are beyond the subject's awareness, hence a daily diary of events may be necessary to identify them. Once identified, their validity can be tested and alternatives considered.

The influence of cognitions upon mood has led to the development of cognitive treatments for depressive illnesses. Depression and the cognitions which are associated with it are regarded as having a circular relationship with one another. The therapist sets behavioural tasks which will demonstrate the irrationality of these cognitions and so reduce their depressive influence. At the same time, success in the behavioural task demonstrates the validity of alternative points of view.

In other neurotic disorders cognitive methods have become increasingly popular. Relevant cognitions range from the understandable fear of impending mental and physical ill health that occur in anxious and phobic subjects to the quite bizarre ideas that may be observed in some obsessive-compulsive disorders. Treatment merges with exposure therapy in its use of behavioural tasks to test the validity of cognitions and *paradoxical* prescriptions are sometimes indicated. Hence, the subject who fears that his anxiety will cause a heart attack may be instructed to practise having heart attacks. Thus far, the efficacy of cognitive methods in the treatment of neurotic disorders in general remains to be established and they may have little, if any, advantage over traditional behavioural treatments.

- **Summary**
Behaviour therapy is an empirically-derived form of psychological treatment whose effectiveness has been demonstrated in a range of human disorders. It is distinguished by a characteristic symptom-orientated approach and by its emphasis upon the current determinants of the clinical problem rather than its historical antecedents. Treatment is often a matter of commonsense and follows logically from an accurate functional analysis.

The treatment of neurotic disorders is a collaborative process in which the subject directs his own treatment with guidance from the therapist. The subject is responsible for completing negotiated task assignments and for maintaining a daily record from which treatment progress can be assessed. In most cases a flexible, multi-technique approach is used.

- **References and Further Reading**
Cobb J., McDonald R., Marks I. et al. (1980) Marital versus exposure therapy: psychological treatments of co-existing marital and phobic–obsessive problems. *Behav. and Modif.* **4**, 3–16.
Liberman R. P. (1972) *A Guide to Behavioural Analysis and Therapy*. Pergamon, New York.
Marks I. M. (1978) *Living with Fear*. McGraw-Hill, New York.
Munby M., Johnston D. W. (1980) Agoraphobia: the long-term follow-up of behavioural treatment. *Brit. J. Psychiat.* **137**, 418–427.
Stern R. S. (1978) *Behavioural Techniques*. Academic Press, London.

Further Reading

Blosh S. (1979) *An Introduction to the Psychotherapies*. Oxford University Press, Oxford.

Brown D. and Pedder, J. (1979) *Introduction to Psychotherapy*. Tavistock Publications, London.

Lomas P. (1973) *True and False Experience*. Alan Lane, London.

Rippere V. and Williams R. (1985) *The Wounded Healer*. Wiley, Chichester.

Storr A. (1979) *The Art of Psychotherapy*. Secker and Warburg and Heinemann Medical, London.

Index